READ ON —
A CONFERENCE APPROACH TO READING

DAVID HORNSBY
and
DEBORAH SUKARNA
with
JO-ANN PARRY

Heinemann
Portsmouth, NH

HEINEMANN EDUCATIONAL BOOKS, INC.
361 Hanover Street
Portsmouth, NH 03801
Offices and agents throughout the world

Library of Congress Cataloging-in-Publication Data

Hornsby, David.
    Read on: a conference approach to reading/David
Hornsby and Deborah Sukarna with Jo-Ann Parry. — 1st
U.S. ed.
    p. cm.
    Includes bibliographies.
    ISBN 0-435-08459-3
    1. Reading (Elementary) — United States. I. Sukarna,
Deborah. II. Parry, Jo-Ann. III. Title.
LB1573.H49 1988
372.4'1— dc19   87-22938
                                        CIP

Printed in the United States of America

CONTENTS

PREFACE

This book is a companion volume to *Write On: A Conference Approach to Writing* (Parry & Hornsby, 1985).

Read On: A Conference Approach to Reading was written for several reasons.

Firstly, there had been a definite trend towards the use of 'real literature' as the core of many reading programs in schools and many teachers were asking us for references. The trend, or rather the *return* to 'real literature', is gaining momentum, but few practical references are available.

Secondly, a single chapter in *Write On* could not possibly cover the topic adequately and we wanted to share some of our experiences with other teachers. We only felt confident to tackle such a task because children in many classrooms had taught us much about reading and writing, particularly the children in Debbie Sukarna's room.

We hope that *Read On: A Conference Approach to Reading* is a practical book. The practices recommended are based on sound theory, which has been presented where appropriate. For those who wish to consider theoretical positions more carefully, further reading lists are provided at the end of each chapter.

We hope that teachers *will* find this a practical book.

We wish to thank the teachers who supported and encouraged us, particularly those who wrote about their classrooms — Jill Holmes, Sue Sparkes, Russell Feben and Kay Sagar. We would also like to thank Colleen Hornsby, who not only read and commented upon the manuscript, but also fed us while we were writing!

Special thanks to all the children who have shown us that this approach can and does work! Comments from some of the children have been quoted throughout the book.

I like the beginning when we read and talk about books all together. It makes you feel like going back and reading.

I like U.S.S.R. because you can concentrate because no one is allowed to disturb anyone.

I think conferences are good because if you are having trouble you just go to Mrs Sukarna and the kids and they will help you and you go away filled with lots of ideas in your head.

I like conferences because you share your book with Mrs Sukarna. I don't really like activities because I would prefer to go on reading.

I like Share Time because I like sharing my books that I read.

I think I'm going OK because at the start of the year I didn't like reading. Now I like it.

Justin

NOTE FOR UNITED STATES READERS

Ages and year levels differ from state to state in Australia. In Victoria (and in this book), they are as follows:

- Prep

  First year at school (many children have had a year at kindergarten or preschool first). Generally children will be 5 years old through most of the year. Legally, children don't have to start until age 6, but they may start school as early as 4½, as regulations say that a child must be 5 by the end of June—which is half way through the school year.

- Year 1

  Second year at school. Generally a child will be 6 years old for most of the year.

- Year 2

  Third year at school (etc.).

  The school year starts at the beginning of February and goes through to mid-December.

1 A CONFERENCE APPROACH TO READING

Characteristics

A conference approach to reading involves the teacher in discussing with the children what they have read; it involves teaching by modelling the art of asking questions, listening to others in a group, discussing issues and showing appreciation of other points of view.

The conference approach has three major characteristics:

- it is literature-based (literature is defined very broadly and the components are discussed in chapter 2);
- it is dependent upon individual and small-group conferences (see chapter 7 in particular);
- it is individualized and the children:
  select their own books;
  are allowed to pace their own progress;
  are encouraged to self-evaluate their work (see chapter 12).

This does not, however, preclude the teacher from providing reading materials or recommending books, or from monitoring or evaluating the progress of each child.

Holdaway (1980, p.40) defines individualized reading as 'a pattern of classroom organization within which different methods of teaching may be used depending on the needs of different children, and the style of the particular teacher'.

We are talking about an **approach** which can incorporate the best of many 'methods' depending upon the children's needs at the time. Teachers who align themselves with any one 'method' are restricting the ways in which they might be responding to children's needs. It is totally inappropriate to believe that 'I am a language-experience teacher' or 'I am a phonics teacher' or 'I am a "look-and-say" teacher and levels are important'. Teachers need to understand and use the best strategies that all methods have to offer. In order to do this, **the same classroom structure and patterns of organization operate for every child.**

It is important to understand that an individualized program does *not* mean that individual programs are run for each child. Every child follows the same routines. It is an individualized program because children are free to select much of their reading material; they self-pace and take responsibility for their progress through materials; they have a say in the 'pressures to perform'; they are responsible for keeping particular records and are involved in their own evaluation. Being involved with the teacher in such decisions helps them to become more independent, and an important aim of education is being achieved.

The approach requires prior organization and planning by the teacher, and methods of doing this, with examples, are provided in chapters 4 and 5 and throughout other chapters.

Overview

Each of the components in a conference-oriented literature-based reading program is explained in more detail in successive chapters. What follows here is a brief overview of the program.

Components in Reading Session

- Introductory Activity
  whole class
  see chapter 5

- Silent Reading
  whole class
  includes the teacher!

- Responding to Reading
  individuals and groups
  see chapters 6, 7 and 8

- Share Time
  whole class
  see chapter 8

The organization of the reading session is detailed in chapter 4. The teacher's timetable follows the components listed above and the children can expect a particular routine to be followed.

The length of each component will vary according to year level and the children's experience with such a program. For example, the silent reading time in a first-year program may be only 3 or 4 minutes, but it is just as important!

> To develop children's ability to **quietly enjoy books,** such time spent with picture-story books, alphabet books, nursery rhyme books, and so on, is essential even in the first year of school.

Introductory Activities

A successful reading classroom functions best when it becomes a 'reading community'. The actual act of reading, like writing, is a solitary activity and the children and teacher must be given a chance to share with others.

For this reason, the reading session commences with an introductory activity with the whole class together. During this time, one of the teacher's main roles is to build a 'reading community' which is supportive and to open the world of children's literature to the children.

So that the introductory activities are not ad hoc, there will be a focus for the week, just as there is for a writing workshop (see companion volume *Write On: A Conference Approach to Writing*).

Silent Reading

The emphasis in a 'conference approach' to reading is on silent reading. Although, as Holdaway points out, the choice is not really between silent and oral reading. Rather, it should be between

PERSONAL READING and AUDIENCE READING

Personal reading may be oral or silent. Beginning readers will often read orally even when they don't need to.

However, even beginning readers should be 'advised' that they too can read 'quietly in their heads', as they often simply don't realize that this is possible! (There seems to be some need, not fully understood at present, for beginning readers to actually pronounce or sub-vocalize words.)

During Silent Reading time, everyone, including the teacher will be reading. Teachers often use this as the USSR (Uninterrupted Sustained Silent Reading) time or the DEAR (Drop Everything And Read) time.

> It is *essential* that the teacher spends some time quietly reading his or her own material.
> **Teacher modelling** is often much more powerful than we realize.

If teachers request the children to read, and then go off and mark their rolls or tidy their desks or put up displays, the message to the children is that the teacher doesn't believe that reading is really all that important!

It has been said that children are not sent to piano teachers who do not play the piano. It is a pity if they are sent to schools where teachers are rarely (if ever!) seen to read or write. The message conveyed by our behaviour must be congruent with the message we articulate.

Responding to Reading

Issues to do with reader response are discussed in chapter 6.

Chapter 7 discusses, in detail, the conference as an important means of responding to reading. Chapter 8 discusses response through activities and sharing.

Conferences

The reading conference, like the writing conference, is the most important component of the program. **It is the best means of harnessing and extending verbal response.**

During the conference, children also have opportunities to

- ask questions
- listen to others
- deepen their understanding
- appreciate others' points of view
- make further re-constructions of author's meanings
- make connections and discover themes.

That is, they will have opportunities to develop their comprehension.

During the conference, children will also attend to aspects of characterization, setting, plot, theme, style, mood and form.

Towards the end of the conference, further related readings may be discussed or recommended and children will be helped with record keeping, self-evaluation and the setting of goals or directions.

Continued Silent Reading

It is important that the children are given the option to continue reading. What could be more infuriating than to be required to shut a book and 'do an exercise or activity' just when you have reached the climax of the book you are reading. If you are just about to turn over the page and 'see if the butler did it or not', and the teacher tells everyone to close their books and start exercises or activities, then the frustration caused will hardly lead to developing an enjoyable reading session. Neither will it encourage the children to become engrossed in a book during the next session.

Activities

The children may respond to reading by engaging in activities that follow naturally from the material read. An activity may be completed for only one in every three or four books read. Also, activities should help children respond more personally and increase their involvement with the story. The activity may be self-chosen, initiated by a group of children, or teacher-required.

Activity time allows children to respond to what they have read in many and varied forms (see chapter 8). However, it is not suggested that overt or 'industrious' response is always essential.

In terms of response, what more could the teacher ask for than:

the tears in the eyes of children who have just listened to *The Happy Prince* by Oscar Wilde.

the subvocal expressions of shock as Abigail is grabbed by a 'frightful thing grinning gap-toothed at her' (*Playing Beatie Bow* by Ruth Park).

the squeals of delight as the teacher reads the text and shows the pictures of *Rosie's Walk* by Pat Hutchins.

Teaching Group

During the teaching group, the teacher and children may attend to 'skills' of reading, such as comprehension of text, oral reading skills, word identification skills and study skills (see Chapter 9).

Of course, these skills are often discussed during the conference sessions. However, the active *listening* role of the teacher during the conference now becomes more specifically a *teaching* role, with some direct instruction. It is during the conference that the teacher discovers what to emphasize in the teaching groups.

Share Time

As already stated in the section on 'Introductory Activities', a successful reading classroom functions best when it becomes a 'reading community'.

A spirit of co-operation and sharing must be built up in all classrooms and must operate throughout the day, and there are many opportunities during the reading session to develop this 'community'.

Children's responses to reading can be shared with others during the whole-class 'Share Time' at the end of each session. When children share their enthusiasms for books, the effect is contagious. When a particular title has been shared, it is often the case that other children immediately want to read that title. Teachers have reported this happening time and time again. Teachers should be pleased that peer recommendations are so powerful and should capitalize on this.

Share Time is for 'publication' of responses to reading — a time to celebrate!

Program Chart

The chart (below) gives an overview of a literature-based reading program.

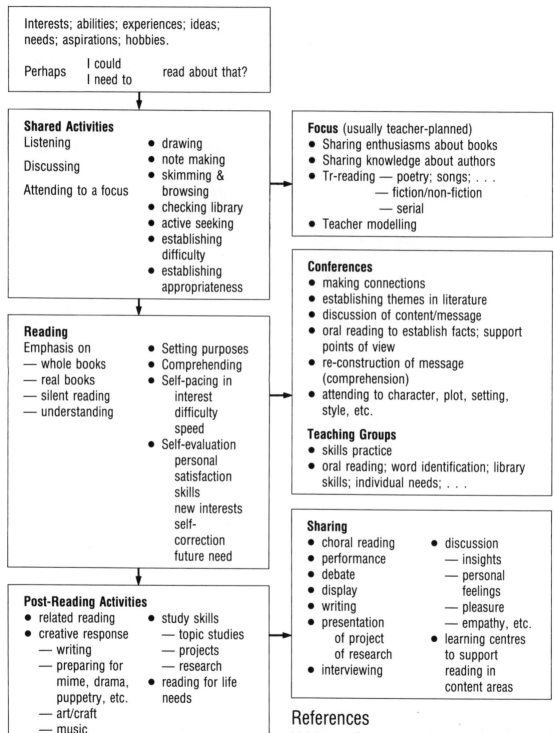

Interests; abilities; experiences; ideas; needs; aspirations; hobbies.

Perhaps   I could / I need to   read about that?

Shared Activities
Listening
Discussing
Attending to a focus
- drawing
- note making
- skimming & browsing
- checking library
- active seeking
- establishing difficulty
- establishing appropriateness

Focus (usually teacher-planned)
- Sharing enthusiasms about books
- Sharing knowledge about authors
- Tr-reading — poetry; songs; . . .
  — fiction/non-fiction
  — serial
- Teacher modelling

Reading
Emphasis on
— whole books
— real books
— silent reading
— understanding
- Setting purposes
- Comprehending
- Self-pacing in
  interest
  difficulty
  speed
- Self-evaluation
  personal
  satisfaction
  skills
  new interests
  self-correction
  future need

Conferences
- making connections
- establishing themes in literature
- discussion of content/message
- oral reading to establish facts; support points of view
- re-construction of message (comprehension)
- attending to character, plot, setting, style, etc.

Teaching Groups
- skills practice
- oral reading; word identification; library skills; individual needs; . . .

Post-Reading Activities
- related reading
- creative response
  — writing
  — preparing for mime, drama, puppetry, etc.
  — art/craft
  — music
- audience reading
- study skills
  — topic studies
  — projects
  — research
- reading for life needs

Sharing
- choral reading
- performance
- debate
- display
- writing
- presentation of project of research
- interviewing
- discussion
  — insights
  — personal feelings
  — pleasure
  — empathy, etc.
- learning centres to support reading in content areas

References

Holdaway, D., *Independence in Reading*, 2nd edn; Ashton Scholastic, 1980.

2 CHILDREN'S LITERATURE

The Extent of Children's Literature

Children's literature is defined very broadly and includes

poetry

plays

novels

words of songs

short stories

picture-story books

non-fiction   anecdotes

the children's own writing

It can be both oral and written. The oral language generated by the children and recorded by the teacher is a form of literature; thus the conference approach is appropriate in the experience-based strand of the program (see chapter 3).

The literature can also include non-English material and the conference approach can be used to great advantage with children speaking languages other than English.

Towards a Definition

'A book is a good book for children only when they enjoy it; a book is a poor book for children, even when adults rate it a classic, if children are unable to read it or are bored by its content.' (Sutherland & Arbuthnot, 1977, p.5)

'The acquisition of skills, including the ability to read, becomes devalued when what one has learned to read adds nothing of importance to one's life.' (Bettleheim, 1976)

'The province of literature is the human condition; life with all its feelings, thoughts, and insights.' (Huck, 1979, p.4)

The experience of literature always involves both the book and the reader. The reader is not passive but is involved in a transaction with the book and its author. The strength or quality of the transactions which occur between the author and the reader provide a measure of the success of the material. (See chapter 6.) **If there is no transaction, there is no experience of literature.**

'Real literature' is written by 'real authors' and provides possibilities for transactions between reader, book and author to occur. 'Real literature' adds to the quality of one's life; it arouses feelings, stimulates thought and develops insights. How do the materials of many published reading schemes measure up? Even literature considered to be 'classic' may not be literature for children. For example, Huck (1979) believes that children may not experience literature when reading Carroll's *Alice in Wonderland* if they have no background in fantasy, if they cannot comprehend the complex plot, or if they cannot tolerate the 'logic of its illogic'.

Why Literature?

Children's literature must be the *core* of every reading program because it is real literature which touches the lives of children in special ways and it is real literature that is asked for time and time again. With real literature, children don't just learn *how* to read; they *choose* to read.

Margaret Meek (1982) writes:

' . . . what the beginning reader reads makes all the difference to his view of reading. For very young beginners, reading is a kind of play, something you do because you like it. . . . Real readers discover how to be more than themselves. The natural way to do this is to sink into a story.' (p.11)

She then goes on to say that the view of reading children accept is the one their first teacher gives them. *So the material used even from the first day of the first year at school must constitute 'real literature'.* It must be something that children can 'sink into'; something that will put another world inside their head. It must engage their imaginations and stir their emotions so that they will laugh, feel sad or sit in wonder. It must extend their understandings.

Why do so many Reading Schemes Fail?

The text of many basic reading schemes currently in use in schools is *not* real literature. However, some recent schemes have improved dramatically, particularly for the 'middle' and 'upper' levels of the primary school. (See list of appropriate schemes and materials at the end of chapter 3.) But the text in the early levels of reading schemes is often constructed by putting together inane strings of letters and words in the belief that it is easier for children to read.

Maurice Saxby has written that the raw material of literature is experience. About reading schemes, he says:

'Debasement is left to those who write not from or about experience as it is, but from socially circumscribed experience measured out by readability scales, graded vocabulary and controlled sentences. Many reading schemes exist to control experience, not broaden it or give it radiance. The practising of scales must not be confused with the playing of a concerto.' (1983, p.11)

McVitty (1982, p.134) describes much of the material used in schools as follows:

- it lacks the excitement and mystery of things outside the child's everyday experience (dogs don't talk; cows don't jump over the moon);
- controlled vocabularies mean that children are not challenged by jaw-breaking words; they don't have a chance to enjoy words such as stegosaurus and diplodocus (as in *Meg's Eggs* by Helen Nicoll);
- it is dull, boring and even an insult to the children's intelligence and imagination; it may be conveniently packaged in levels, but is innocuous.

The materials used must contain these ingredients, but they are often missing. The materials must be *memorable* and they must attract readers again and again. Adults do not remember the distorted text of early 'readers' they may have plodded through at school, but if they were lucky enough to have real literature to read, much of it will be remembered fondly. For example, the Victorian Education Department 'readers' of the fifties contained real literature. Many remember *The Hobyahs* from the Grade 2 'reader' or *Lazy Tok* from the Grade 3 'reader'. **Literature was the core of the reading program.**

What teacher or parent has ever had a child ask 'Please may I have "Nan can fan Dan" again?' Or 'Please will you read me that book which goes "In here? No. In here? No. In here? No?"' But teachers and parents have been asked *again and again* to read such books

as *The Three Billy Goats Gruff* or *The Three Bears* or any selection from the *Mother Goose* treasury. They have had children joining in with them to say, 'Hundreds of cats, thousands of cats, millions and billions and trillions of cats.' *A child's reading experience begins with these well-loved favourites and must continue with them. This is the real stuff of reading. Children don't need fake material and neither do teachers!*

The Use of Selected Reading Scheme Materials

While most reading schemes fail miserably at the lower levels, some of the more recent ones have upper levels which *do* contain good selections of literature, which are well presented and which lead children to other literature. Many are thematic and combine selections or extracts that have common links or connections. When schemes also focus on specific areas of content, they are not just 'readers', but valuable resource books for social studies and science.

If reading schemes are to be used, they should be chosen very carefully, with attention being given to the nature and organization of the material.

Remember also that a reading scheme can only be one strand of a reading program and *must* be balanced by a wide variety of other materials. These will include materials such as magazines, reference books, comics, newspapers, anthologies, child-produced materials and books in community languages.

Why Self-Choice of Reading Material?

It is *essential* that children be allowed to choose much of their reading material. When children choose:

- they learn to select books which suit their interests, needs and abilities
- they become more discerning
- they learn to choose wisely
- they don't need 'teacher-motivation' to make them read.

Also, it is a common trait of human behaviour that we attend more carefully and willingly to the things we have chosen for ourselves. When we have been involved in a decision, we are more likely to involve ourselves in the resulting action or behaviour; we will be more enterprising, enthusiastic, industrious and persevering.

More than ever before, children need to realize that reading *is* a worthwhile choice. Television and modern entertainment, while valuable, tend to dominate choice because they are there and their presence is a strong one. Teachers need to show children that reading is also something that *they* choose to do.

Another important reason for encouraging children to choose their own materials is that we want them to become independent in as many ways as possible. A daily aim of education is to have children become more and more independent, but they will remain *dependent* if decisions are always made for them. Even from their first day at school, children must be given many opportunities to make decisions and to work out courses of action for themselves. (Never do for children what they can do for themselves!) Independence is not something that just happens at the end of the primary school years; it is something that is developed daily.

Early Choices may not be Wise Ones

When children are first given the opportunity to choose their own material, their choices may not be wise ones, especially if they have had years of material being prescribed for them.

However, children can only learn to choose wisely when they are given the *opportunity* to choose.

Returning a poorly chosen book and replacing it with a more appropriate one is a sign of development, not failure.

When children are free to choose their own books, many of the 'motivation-to-read' problems are vastly reduced, if not eliminated. **The rewards of a book are seen to lie within the covers of the book itself.** External motivation and rewards for reading are used in much the same way as bells were used to make dogs salivate! Use *books* to get children reading, not stars, smiles and free time.

Teacher's Role

Even though the children are often free to choose their own reading materials, this does not mean that the teacher has no role to play. In fact, the opposite is true. Teachers must be providing a rich literature environment in the classroom; they must be introducing the children to many authors and titles; they must be giving daily invitations to discover the rewards within the covers.

Discover Literature Together!

If you, the teacher, are one of the many who have learned to read but not to love reading, then you will also need to immerse yourself in children's literature. As you discover it, share your discoveries with the children. Make a pact to discover together!

Start reading now! Try 'A Taste of Blackberries or Bridge to Terabithia if you want your feelings stirred; The Silver Sword or I Am David if you want to take part in some personal journeys; The Great Gilly Hopkins, The Witch of Blackbird Pond or The Slave Dancer to meet with further suffering and problems caused by prejudice. Above all, these books (and many, many others) allow you to enter other people's worlds. They are to be relished, possessed, wallowed in. In them, you will recognize people and places you know, gain new understandings, detect aspects of yourself in others, witness personal feelings that are usually hidden, explore relationships between people and learn of things you never even imagined. Share this with the children; help them to make discoveries too!

Another discovery will be that literature is useful right across the curriculum. You will discover that literature is enjoyable and then you will have acquired the most important single trait of the successful reading teacher.

References

Bettleheim, B., *The Uses of Enchantment: Meaning and Importance of Fairy Tales*, Alfred A. Knopf, Inc., 1976.

Carpenter, H. & Pritchard, M., *The Oxford Companion to Children's Literature*, Oxford University Press, 1984.

Fader, D. et al., *Hooked on Books*, 10th Anniversary Edition, Berkley Medallion Book, 1976.

Huck, C., *Children's Literature in the Elementary School*, Holt, Rinehart and Winston, 3rd edn. updated, 1979.

McVitty, W., (ed.), *Word Magic: Poetry as a Shared Adventure*, Primary English Teaching Association, 1985.

Meek, M., *Learning to Read*, The Bodley Head, 1982.

Saxby, M., 'What is Literature?' in Walshe, et al., (eds.), *Teaching Literature*, Primary English Teaching Association, 1983.

Sutherland, Z. & Arbuthnot, M., *Children and Books*, 5th Edn, Scott Foresman, 1977.

3 A BALANCED READING PROGRAM

Three Interdependent Strands

In chapter 1, a conference approach to reading has been very briefly outlined. This program is appropriate even from week one of the first year at school and will include introductory activities, discussion groups about a particular picture book or picture-story book which has been read by the teacher or heard using a listening-post, a few minutes (or more!) quietly enjoying self-chosen books, and sharing. It will also incorporate Shared Book Experience and practices we have learned through a Language Experience approach. In chapter 2, the importance of using 'real literature' has been emphasized.

This chapter will show how a 'graded text' strand and an 'experience-based' strand may be incorporated and how they must be *interdependent* with the 'literature strand' of the program.

These strands refer mainly to the types of **materials** that will be used. They are *not* independent strands and have many overlaps. For example, the books from the graded text strand will be literature-based or non-fiction materials which could often be used as materials in the other two strands.

A Balanced Reading Program

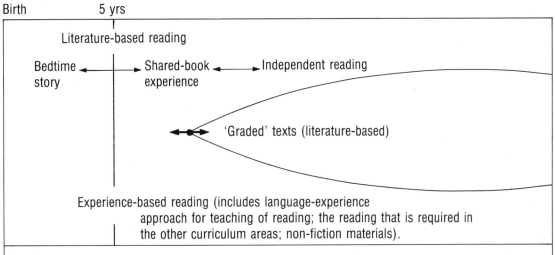

Birth   5 yrs

Literature-based reading

Bedtime ◄──────► Shared-book ◄──────► Independent reading
story   experience

◄──●──► 'Graded' texts (literature-based)

Experience-based reading (includes language-experience
approach for teaching of reading; the reading that is required in
the other curriculum areas; non-fiction materials).

The point shown ◄──●──► will move backwards or forwards in time depending on the graded material being used and how it is used. For example, an early book from 'Story Box' (Rigby) could be used for shared-book experience on the first day of school, but the earliest Core Library books (Ashton Scholastic) might not be used until the second or third year at school.

Adapted from Holdaway, 1980.

Three Interdependent Strands

Literature Strand

The individually chosen literature (from simple picture story books to multiple copies of quality children's literature) will be an important strand of the program and the teacher will need to hold shared-book activities and conferences with the children about their reading material.

Experience-Based Reading

A second strand is the experience-based reading. This includes the well-known language-experience procedures. (A 'language-experience approach' would more correctly be called a 'reading-experience approach' since it emphasizes the teaching/learning of reading rather than writing/composing. For a discussion of this issue, see the companion volume to this text, *Write On: A Conference Approach to Writing*, 1985, p. 71.) The experience-based strand also includes the reading that is built into the writing program, and the reading of non-fiction materials (including those used for other curriculum areas, particularly science and social studies).

'Graded' Texts

A third strand will be the use of graded texts.

The graded texts must still be literature-based. This means that in general they must have been written by *authors* who want to tell a *story*; not by publishers who may have destroyed text in the name of making material 'easier'.

For a list of some of the graded materials considered suitable, see the end of this chapter.

Use of 'Basic Readers'

Teachers are often convinced of the use of literature as a main strand of their reading program, but can find themselves in a school that has committed itself (often for non-educational reasons) to a particular reading scheme.

When this is the case, teachers should identify those selections that have literary merit and use them. There is certainly no need to 'do' every selection and the authors of such schemes never intended that anyway.

Fortunately, some published reading schemes have improved much in recent years and have returned, in the main, to use of real literature and informational selections. When the content of these books is also based on a theme or common focus, then the books can often be used to link reading with other areas of the curriculum.

Using the Selections with Literary Merit

Johnson and Louis, in their book *Literacy Through Literature* (Methuen, 1985) suggest alternative ways of using the selections that have literary merit. They recommend the following procedures, which are particularly useful with lower primary grades but are also relevant to groups right through the primary school.

1 Reading to the children
The *teacher* reads the chosen selection to the children with expression and natural intonation.

2 Joining in
The children are encouraged to join in as the text becomes familiar.

3 Framing
Framing of lines, phrases or words is used when the teacher or children want to emphasize these segments of texts.

4 Comprehension activities
Many game type activities are described in Johnson and Louis' book, such as 'lies and clues', which are useful for developing comprehension.

5 Word activities
Again, game type activities, such as 'substitutions' and 'Spoonerisms', are used to give closer attention to words.

6 Unison reading
When children are familiar with the selection and it is one of many in their repertoire, then it will be 're-visited' by way of unison reading. Johnson and Louis recommend that, as new stories are added to the repertoire, earlier stories are dropped, so that the repertoire is maintained at four or five stories.

Holdaway puts the proper use of graded texts into another perspective:

'As children become conscious of their ability to decode print, it is important to make available to them caption readers and other simplified books, which they can handle independently at a sitting — say, in five minutes. This seems to us the proper use of graded materials, rather than to attempt to use them as instructional material. We remember that we are committed to using a captivating literature in which literature prediction can operate at a deep level, and then we provide a wealth of more simple material upon which children can cut their teeth as independent readers. But, heaven forbid giving any child one of those linguistically mangled texts which have been designed to introduce words or phonetic elements in a so-called rational progression. "Ratty on the Matty" is out.'
(1979. p.77)

All three strands of the reading program will include procedures commonly used by teachers, such as:
- shared writing/reading activities (for example, Wall Stories)
- the use of Big Books
- teacher reading *to* the children
- U.S.S.R. or any procedure for encouraging silent reading
- cued reading
- choral reading
- directed reading-thinking activities.

Consequently, reading 'skills' are taught through all three strands.

A Selection of Suitable 'Graded' Materials

There is a great wealth of literature-based materials available for classroom use today. Teachers no longer have to rely on anything less. The materials listed below certainly do not constitute a complete list. 'Series' or 'schemes' are referred to when the majority of the titles are literature-based; some individual books within the schemes may not qualify as 'good literature' and teachers should be selective. Only the classroom teacher knows the children well enough to make final judgements. If certain books 'fail' with the children, take the opportunity to talk with them about that and help them make comparisons with books they love.

'Story Box' materials (Rigby)
– Read Togethers (for Shared-Book experience)

'Story Chest' (Rigby)

'Story Starters' (Rigby)

'Rigby Theme Packs'
– for emergent readers and writers
– books written *with* children *for* children
– 4 themes: 5 titles in each (one big book)
  'Animals'
  'Food'
  'Families'
  'School'

'Young Australia' (Nelson)
– levels 7 to 17 and Extension levels A & B contain a wide range of literature (Extension C & D in preparation)

'Story Strand' of 'Young Australia' (Nelson)
– 4 titles at each level

The New 'Ready to Read' series (Nelson)
– shared reading
– guided reading
– independent reading

'Windmill Books' (Nelson)
– 'Rhyme and Rhythm' books
– 'Alan Wagstaff's Alphabet'
– 'Look and Listen' Set A
– 'Look and Listen' Set B

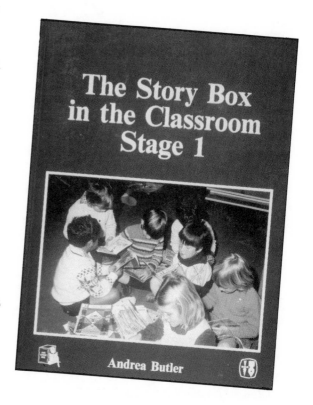

The Story Box in the Classroom Stage 1

Andrea Butler

City Kids and *Country Kids* books (Nelson)
— Lorraine Wilson's well-known and well-loved books.

Ginn Reading Program:
– familiar nursery rhymes (4-6 yrs)
– 'Fables from Aesop' (5-7 yrs)
– 'Look At . . .' books (5-8 yrs)
– 'Once Upon A Time' books (5-8 yrs)
– 'Whatever Next?' books (6-8 yrs)
– 'Thunder the Dinosaur' books (6-9 yrs)
– 'Tales from Long Ago' books (7-9 yrs)
– 'Watching' books/non-fiction (7-12 yrs)
– 'Animals on the Move' books/non-fiction (8-10 yrs)
– 'The Changing Earth' books/non-fiction (8-12 yrs)
– 'Traditional Tales from Around the World' (9-14 yrs)

'Young Puffins':
– 'Read Alouds' for reading to children
– 'Read Alones' for first solo reading and building confidence
– 'Story Books' for children developing reading stamina

'Puffinpacks' (selected Puffin titles)
– lower primary level
– middle primary level
– upper primary level

'Readalong Rhythms' (Ashton Scholastic)
– Big Book collections
– 5 sets (4 titles in each)

'Read It Again' series (Ashton Scholastic)
– big books
– 3 levels

'Giant Books' (Methuen)
– *Gobble Gobble Glup Glup*
– *The Three Little Pigs*
– *The Little Red Hen*

'Australian Animals' (Methuen)
– excellent non-fiction, high-interest series
– full colour photographs
– sets 1,2 & 3 cover Prep to Year 3
– 8 titles in each set

'Planet Earth' (Methuen)
– 4 sets with 4 titles in each
– *Dinosaurs*
– *Wild Animals*
– *Technology*
– *Space*
– Prep to Year 3

'Super Springers' (Methuen)
– poems, songs, rhymes and chants
– 4 large-format books for Prep to Year 2

'Kangaroo Creek' (Methuen)
– Starters for Prep level
– Australian theme

'Kangaroo Creek Gang' (Methuen)
– Year 1
– Australian theme

'Beginnings' (Methuen)
– designed for 4-6 year olds
– 12 large full colour books for shared reading
– 4 full colour wall stories
– 5 full colour wall posters
– wide variety of literature

'Project Australia' (Methuen)
– listed as Social Studies books but would be
   excellent material for reading program

'Choices' (Methuen)
– Choices 4, Years 5, 6, 7
– Choices 3
– Choices 1-2 to be published
– a literature-based reading and writing
   program

'Banana Books' (Heinemann)
– bright, imaginative stories
– bridge between picture-story books and
   novels
– for 7-10 year olds

Oxford University Press:
– 'Umbrella Books' for 5-7 year olds
– 'Eagle Books' for 8-12 year olds
– 'Archway Novels' for 11+ years
– picture-story books by Brian Wildsmith
– 'Read-a-Lot' books

'Gazelle Books' (Hamish Hamilton)
– for 5-8 year olds
– simple but complete stories
– transition from picture-story books to novels

'Antelope Books' (Hamish Hamilton)
– for 6-9 year olds
– lively and original stories
– for children who have begun to enjoy solo
  reading

Hodder & Stoughton:
– 'Grug' books
– 'Hopscotch' series (between picture-story
  books and novels)
– 'Magnet' books
– 'First Fairy Tales'
– 'Stoat' books
– 'Pocket Bears'

References

Holdaway, D., *The Foundations of Literacy*,
Ashton Scholastic, 1979.
——, *Independence in Reading*, Ashton Scholastic, 2nd edn., 1980.
Johnson, T., & Louis, D., *Literacy Through Literature*, Methuen, 1985.
Parry, J., & Hornsby, D., *Write On: A Conference Approach to Writing*, Martin Educational, 1985.

4 ORGANIZATION AND PLANNING

I enjoy U.S.S.R. (Uninterrupted Sustained Silent Reading) because I'm reading a very interesting book called "What Goes Up, Must come Down". It's really funny and I almost feel like laughing and sometimes I do.

Marnie

I really like it because it gives you time to get stuck into your story. When I get stuck into my story, I really fly.

Brett

Planning of the Reading Session

An overview of the program has been given in Chapter 1. It is important to look at how the teacher will use his or her time in organizing the reading session and it is important that the children learn the routine that the teacher is going to follow. It is impossible to set down a timetable for the children, as they will spend different lengths of time on different activities. However, their activities follow a set pattern: the time allocations for activities may vary, but the routine, and the order in which the activities are done, remains the same.

Any timetable is a suggestion only. It may be altered by teachers, in consultation with the children, until a framework that suits is found to work.

To reiterate, the teacher's pattern is as follows:

- an **Introductory Activity** which is usually developed around a weekly focus
- **Silent Reading** of self-selected material (the teacher *always* reads silently during this time as well)
- a **Conference** session with a group of children while the other children continue to read quietly or commence an activity related to their reading (whether it be their current piece or some previous reading material). The activity may be self-chosen, initiated by a group of children, or teacher-required.
- possibly a **Teaching Group** (that is, a conference to attend to a specific issue or reading skill)
- a whole-class **Share Time** which is used by children to share enthusiasms for books read, to display art/craft responses, to perform or dramatize sections of books, to share what they have learned about authors, and so on.

While this may be the general pattern that the children also follow, not all these aspects of the program will necessarily be attended to by every child in any one session.

Consider the following examples:

Child A: After the whole-class introductory activity and the silent reading time, she chooses to continue reading for another 10 minutes until she finishes the chapter she is reading from *Moominsummer Madness*. She then continues making puppets for some of the Moomintrolls until the whole class is called together again for Share Time.

Child B: After the whole-class introductory activity and the silent reading time, he joins a conference group with the other three children who have just finished reading *A Wizard of Earthsea*. The purpose of this conference is to check the maps the children did to show Ged's journey from island to island in the Archipelago, to discuss his 'personal journey' of growing up and any other points the children want to make. After the conference, he works with the other children in the group to prepare a large map of Ged's journey to share with the rest of the class at a later date. Then he joins the whole class for Share Time.

Child C: After the whole-class introductory activity and the silent reading time, she continues reading quietly for several minutes. Then she practises reading aloud a section of *The Nimbin* that she has chosen to read orally to the teacher and children in the teaching group. After the teaching group, during which audience reading skills were being attended to, she joins the whole class for the Share Time.

Obviously, it is impossible to set a strict timetable which every child will follow. Nevertheless, what they do does fit into the overall pattern of organization operating in the classroom.

Since it is the *teacher* who follows a more predictable routine, it is better to concentrate on the teacher's use of time. When this routine is followed by the teacher every day, the children *can* predict what is going to happen next. They know what kind of help they can get and

when they can get it. They will know when the teacher is available to them and when they have to wait. When there is no sound routine, children will interrupt the teacher and other children at inconvenient times, and may even 'cruise around' the room (a road to disaster for any individualized program!).

A suggested timetable for years 2-6 might be as follows:
For Prep and Year 1, see page 26.

Introductory activities
- focus for week   10-15 min.
- will often be common focus for both the writing and reading workshops
- teacher planned and directed

Quiet time
- silent reading (*teacher*   5-25 min.
  reading too!)   (depending on
                                        year level and
                              children's experience)

Responding to reading
- conferences   20-25 min.
  (usually groups; sometimes individuals)
- activities related to reading
- more silent reading (children are free to continue reading silently if they wish. A major aim of our program is that they should want to do this!)
- Teaching Groups
- Required Comments/Log Book

Share time
- whole class together again   5-10 min.
- discussion; display; performance; choral reading; etc.
- children take responsibility

When teachers first introduce a conference approach to reading such as that being suggested in this book, the time allocations suggested above may not be appropriate. For example, if the children have not been used to silent reading for any extended periods of time, then this part of the program may be very short. At first, the teacher may require only a few minutes of silent reading. This may be increased to 10 minutes, 15 minutes, 20 minutes . . . the limit being determined by the age of the children, their previous opportunities to read quietly or browse through books, and their growing desire to read for longer periods of time.

Preparation

Physical Environment

The physical set-up of the room is very important. It should be arranged in consultation with the children as they are the ones who will be expected to work independently within it.

It is essential to have an area where the whole class can be seated comfortably for the introductory activity and for the share time at the end of the session; an area where close contact is possible. This area can also be used by the teacher and the conference group.

Make sure there is a table or an area reserved for independent activities. Children can then go to this area whenever necessary. For example, when children are in between books or activities, they can go to that area to choose an independent activity. (Some teachers use learning centres for this purpose.)

Also make sure that there is an activity area which allows for movement and talk. (This may be a space within the classroom itself, or the centre area between two classrooms, or even the corridor!)

Materials

There must be a wide range of reading materials readily available to the children. The selection should include fiction, non-fiction, poetry, children's magazines (such as 'Challenge' and 'Explore') and multiple-copy materials. Don't forget picture-story books! They are relevant to *all* year levels.

The materials required to enable the children to respond appropriately to reading will be many and varied. They will include art/craft materials, magazines, newspapers, cardboard, computer paper, etc. The children will often have worthwhile recommendations to make about the storage of these materials and they should be required to organize and label them. When *they* have responsibility in this area, upkeep rarely becomes a problem for the teacher.

The Teacher and the Children

The teacher *must* be well prepared.

In setting up a program where individual children and groups are required to select their own reading materials and where they are allowed to respond in different ways, the teacher must ensure that organizational issues are worked out *before* the program starts.

The teacher can help the children select materials if something is known of their interests. A knowledge of the children's interests also helps the teacher select titles for bulk borrowing. Consequently, it is useful to have the children fill in 'Interest Inventories'. (A reproducible inventory is included in Appendix 1.)

The teacher should become familiar with the titles in the library and with the librarian's help select a wide variety of materials covering as far as possible the children's interests and beyond. The teacher *must* be a reader.

Remember too, that children can bring reading materials from home to share with others, and municipal libraries will make bulk loans available to schools.

Organization of Books

The books need to be organized in such a way as to be freely accessible to children. The way in which they are displayed is important. A display of book covers is far more enticing than a row of book spines. It not only attracts attention but suggests what will be found inside the covers.

It is often helpful to record the titles of the books on a whole-class chart. This should include two columns in which the children can enter the dates when borrowing and returning books and a third column for their signature. This establishes a routine for the children and helps them to be accountable for what they borrow. It also enables the teacher and the children to keep track of where books are. Such charts could be organized by topics, themes or collected class interests; books which are good for a giggle; hobbies; etc.

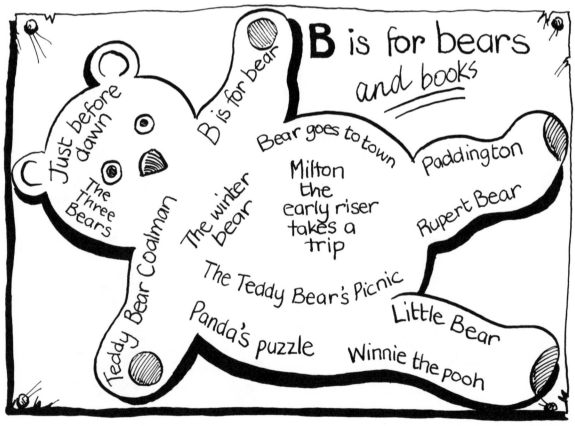

Reading Folders

Each child should be supplied with a manilla folder to keep a record of his or her reading. (For details about keeping records and using them for evaluation see chapter 12.)

In the first year or two at school, these records will be quite simple and assistance from the teacher will be required but, as soon as they are able to do so, the children should start keeping records in the following way:

Front cover:
This should be headed 'Reading Folder' and should also indicate child's name and year. Each child illustrates own cover.

Inside front cover:
Heading: 'Titles I Would Like to Read'
Purpose: to have the children think about the books they might read; to encourage the children to record the titles recommended by others; to provide the children with a resource list when 'stuck' for a title.
Heading: 'Topics I Would Like to Read About'
Purpose: to have the children consider different topics; to record topics suggested by others; to provide a resource list for possible group conferences and related readings.

Inside back cover:
Heading: 'Conferences'
Purpose: to have the children record the date of the conference, the purpose of the conference, and whether it was an individual or group conference. (The purpose may be to consider a common title, common author, common topic or theme, genre, and so on. See chapter 7.)

Inserted sheets:
Purpose: to keep a record of what is read.

These sheets may include 'Books I've Read' where titles and dates can be recorded, and they may include lists of titles from published material that can be used as checklists and dated when read. When children choose to read other material outside school (at home or during holidays) then records of such reading could also be kept. Records of activities completed could also be shown on other sheets.

Reading Folders for Younger Children

The teacher may need to make most of the entries for younger children, but as soon as the children are capable of making their own entries, they must be encouraged and helped to do so. Many variations are possible, but it is important that children get into the habit of thinking about what they are doing and recording what they have done.

Guiding principle: **Never do for children what they can do for themselves.**

Front cover:
Headed 'Reading Folder' and indicating child's name and year. Each child illustrates own cover.

Inside front cover:
Heading: 'My Favourite Books'
Purpose: to have children identify with books positively; to encourage them to think about their responses to books; to raise their awareness and acceptance of individual differences; to indicate their interests to the teacher.

Inside back cover:
Heading: 'My Favourite Friends'
Purpose: to have children think about the characters in books; other purposes as above.

Inserted sheets:
Purpose: to keep a record of material read. These sheets may include 'Books I've Read' where titles and dates are recorded, and they may include lists of titles from published material that can be used as checklists and dated when read.

The children may also be required to respond to the book by colouring in an appropriate face on these sheets:

Children's responses will take many forms and will range from simple colouring in of faces to more sophisticated written responses.

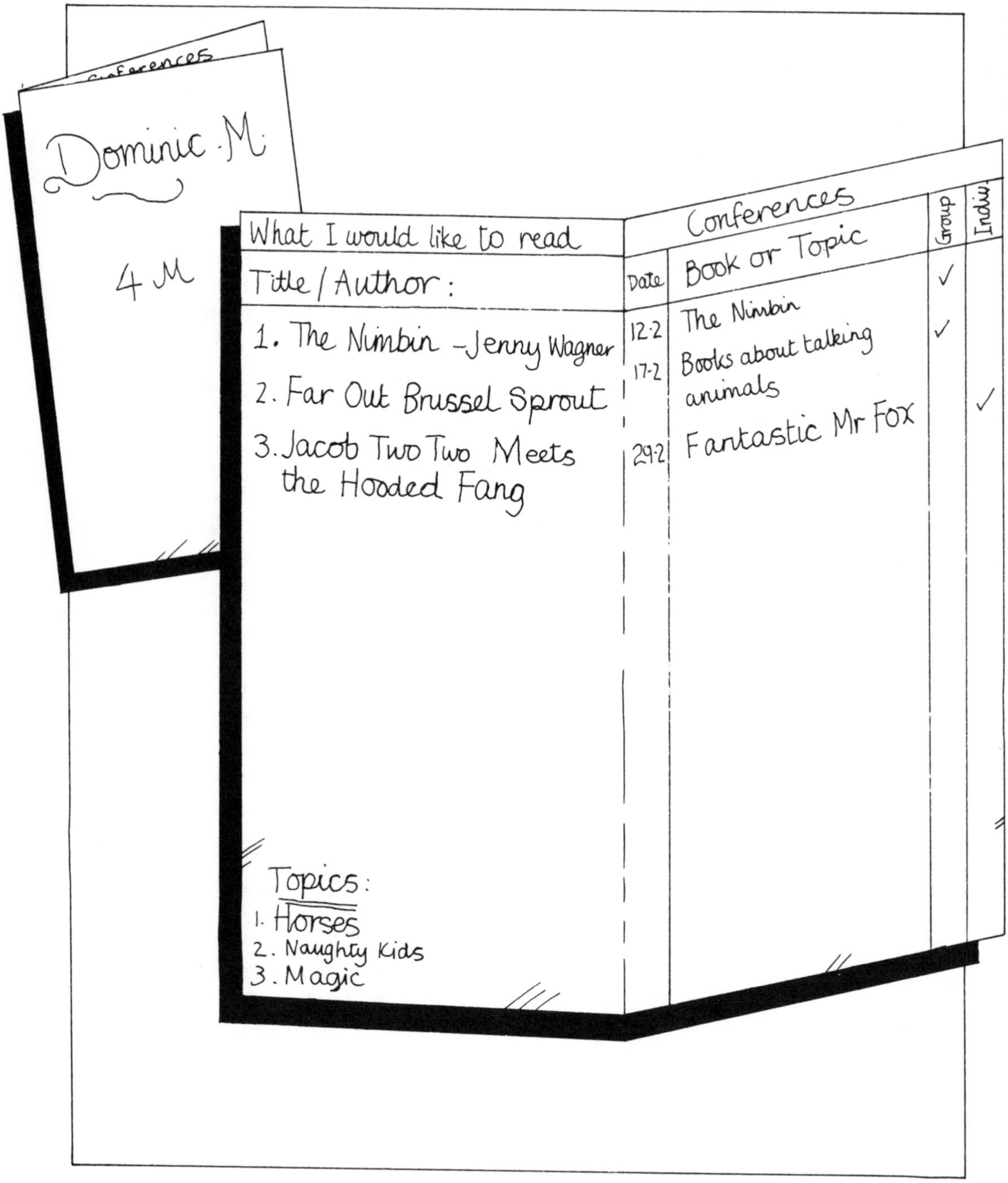

Dominic · M

4 M

Conferences

What I would like to read

Title / Author :

1. The Nimbin – Jenny Wagner
2. Far Out Brussel Sprout
3. Jacob Two Two Meets the Hooded Fang

Topics :
1. Horses
2. Naughty Kids
3. Magic

Date	Book or Topic	Group	Indiv
		✓	
12·2	The Nimbin	✓	
17·2	Books about talking animals		✓
29·2	Fantastic Mr Fox		

Sheets kept inside the folder to record books read. (Teachers sometimes use separate sheets for different materials. For example, a blank sheet for self-chosen materials; a sheet with listed titles for a 'scheme' or program which allows titles to be simply dated when they have been read.)

Books I've Read

Title / Author	Date Started	Date Finished
The Nimbin (J. Wagner)	4·2	10·2
The Elephant and the Bad Baby (E. Vipont)	12·2	12·2
Jeremiah in the dark woods (Ahlberg)	13·2	17·2
Fantastic Mr Fox (Dahl)	20·2	28·2
The Dead Letter Box (J. Mark)	2·3	

Required Comments and the 'Log Book'

In addition to the records that are kept in each child's reading folder, children in years 4, 5 and 6 are generally required to write some form of brief comment. If a separate exercise book or section of a folder is kept for this purpose, the comments become a useful 'Reading Log'.

Some children in Years 2 and 3 are also capable of writing brief comments. Individual teachers will need to use their common sense and knowledge of the children they work with to decide when they will require comments.

Part of the teacher's preparation will include the production of sheets which help to direct the children's comments. Some sample sheets, headed 'Thinking About My Reading', are included in Appendix I as reproducible sheets. They are for fiction books and informational books. **The questions on the sheets are Guiding Questions only.** It is *never* suggested that specific questions should be answered. Often, children will write their own comment (not in response to any of the guiding questions on the sheets at all). The questions are used simply to prompt children about the kinds of comments they might write and should only be needed until the children learn what is involved. With experience, the children will gradually do without the sheets altogether.

The **'Log Book'** entry should commence with the title of the book (or selection) as the heading and information about authors, illustrators and publication. This is followed by the child's own response. The form and length of the child's response will vary according to the book read, the child's comprehension, the child's intention, the teacher's intention, and the purpose for keeping the record.

For details and examples, see the section on 'Required Comments' in chapter 8.

Getting Started

'Selling' Books

It is essential that teachers convey to the children their own interest in, and love of, literature. Teachers could start by sharing with the children a favourite piece of literature they have read. This could be an appropriate time to ask the children how they feel about reading. Their responses will complement the information teachers get from the 'Interest Inventory' and will help to identify those children who may need their assistance in getting started.

'Sell' the books in the classroom collection by:
- reading, as a serial, a 'sure-fire winner' (see chapter 11 for suggestions)
- showing front covers, reading titles, showing illustrations
- reading 'blurbs' from back covers
- mentioning authors and other books they have written
- encouraging children to share any books from home that they have included in the current classroom collection
- reading extracts
- talking about story lines and themes
- relating to real-life experiences
- highlighting personalities.

> Be enthusiastic!
> Be excited about newly acquired books!
> Show your delight!
> Share favourite selections!

Choosing Books

If the children have not been allowed to choose their own reading material before, then their early choices may not be wise ones. The only way children will learn to choose wisely is if they are given opportunities to do so.

It is only after the children know what is in the class collection that self-choice is possible. There may still be one or two children who feel that there is nothing there for them. If so, then the teacher will need to spend extra time with these children — perhaps in the library. The teacher should also check the children's Interest Inventories and discuss them with the children.

Many children don't know how to choose *for themselves*. They choose a book that they think will please the teacher.

> Teachers have to convince these children that reading is primarily for the reader!

The teacher's role includes coaxing, encouraging and persevering. Time and patience on the teacher's part will show the children that the teacher is serious about freedom of choice. When teachers show that they value children's choices and trust in their ability to choose, their capacity to do so develops dramatically. In addition, such trust makes the children feel good about themselves.

Establishing Routines

Prep and Year 1

At the Prep level, and also into Year 1, teachers will need to establish routines, but these will be dependent upon:

- teacher's preferences
- materials to be used
- time given to independent enjoyment of reading materials
- teacher's intention with respect to the various strands of the reading program (see chapter 3).

Teachers of Prep and Year 1 have found that the following routine is often appropriate.

Introductory Activity
- whole class
- could be shared-book experience; wall story; something related to published scheme or program being used; nursery rhymes; language-experience.

Responding to Reading
- activities related to introductory activity (e.g. arranging sentences of language-experience story; completing own copy of wall story; listening post; personal dictionary or word bank entries)

- group conference based on material introduced by the teacher in the Introductory Activity
- activities related to own previous reading
- activities from published programs

Silent Reading
- self-choice from materials in room and 'known' books (books previously introduced by the teacher and now familiar)
- teacher reads silently too!

Share Time
- whole class
- children responsible for sharing

This changed procedure is sometimes more appropriate with the very young children, as activities need to be closely related to the teacher-directed introductory activity in both time and kind. Also, after young children have had time to quietly read or enjoy their own selections, they usually want to talk about it immediately. Hence, Share Time can follow immediately after silent reading time, allowing for 'show and tell'.

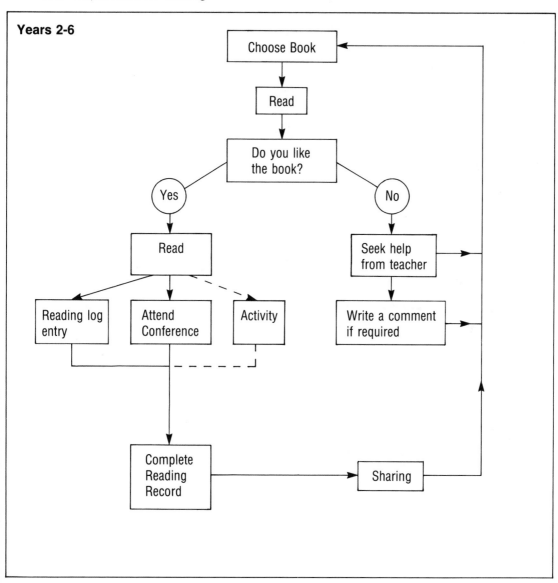

Years 2-6

Samples of Teachers' Work Plans

1   Work Plan for Year 1

Language Workshop – focus on Reading   Week Ending:

Focus for Introductory Activity: *Grandparents*	Name	Conf.	Tchg.Grp	Share T.

Monday
Introductory Activity: *Shared Book*
Read 'Grandpa Grandpa' (Big Book – story box).
Discuss each page (count the items). Re-read
pointing to text. – have children join in.
 	
Responding to Reading: *Independent Activities*
1. Wall story - (text copied on blank sheets). Discuss
   detail for illustrations → children to illustrate.
   Match & sequence text as a group.
2. Listening post → multiple copies of the story.
3. Innovations on text → keep the characters
   but make new sentence structures – teacher
   writes – Big Book.
 	
Silent Reading
Share Time:
Wall Story — different groups explain
their illustrations.
	Nicole	✓		

	Virginia	✓		
	Amy	✓		✓
	Brett		✓	
	Jime		✓	
	Dino		✓	✓
	Trevor		✓	✓

Tuesday
Introductory Activity:
 	
Read: 'grandmother' by Jeannie Baker. Discuss
relationships, illustrations (collage)
 	
Responding to Reading:
1. Listening Post - multiple copies
2. Children writing own stories about what they
   like to do with their grandparents → Teacher
   Conferences / scribes etc.
3. Children illustrate their new story → match &
   sequence text → Big Book.
 	
Silent Reading
 	
Share Time:
Big Book
	Bernice	✓		

	Tania B.		✓	✓
	Melita	✓		
	Diane	✓		
	Nhut		✓	
	Andrew		✓	✓
	John	✓		
	Paul	✓		✓

	Name	Conf.	Tchg.Grp	Share T.
Wednesday Introductory Activity: *Read 'Grandfather' by J. Baker.* *Discuss & compare relationship with 'grandpa grandpa'.* Responding to Reading: *1. Discuss all books related to theme. What do we learn from them? How are the characters like us? etc. Write letter to grandparent (older person) - let them know why you think they're special.* *2. Children finish writing stories/illustrate →independent reading - 'Books we can Read' box.* *3. Listening Post - Multiple Copies* Silent Reading Share Time: *Travis - shared a book that belonged to his grandfather.*	Thang			✓
	Robert			✓
	Wayne	✓		
	Steven	✓		
	Natasha		✓	
	Simone	✓	✓	
	Maria		✓	
	Christine	✓	✓	
Thursday Introductory Activity: *Grandmother invited to speak: 'Mrs. Aday' → talk with children about role of grandmother. What's special about it? Children can ask questions.* Responding to Reading: *Drama – Whole Class* *Re-read: 'Grandpa Grandpa' – big book.* *Children make simple hand actions to go with story → join in reading.* *Dramatise theme of going fishing: rowing out to sea; throwing out the line etc. (music on tape).* Silent Reading Share Time: *Chn. show photographs of g'parents; talk about books they read as chn.*	Tracy			✓
	Sarah	✓		
	Tania S.	✓		
	Debbie	✓		✓
	Travis		✓	
	David		✓	✓
	Joe		✓	✓

2   Work Plan for Years 2-3

Language Workshop – focus on Reading   Week Ending:

Focus for Introductory Activity: *Giants*	Name	Conf.	Tchg. Grp	Share T.
Monday Introductory Activity: *Introduce selection of books which have common theme of 'Giants'. Read:* i *How Big Mouth Wrestled the giant.' Discuss.* Silent Reading Responding to Reading: *Conference group: 'The Story of Ferdinand'.* – *Martin, Casey, Jane* 1. *Story Telling. What makes a good story? Discuss art of story telling. List main points in 'Jack & the Beanstalk' for retelling. Prepare to tell class* Share Time: *Keith: Mobile of jungle creatures* *Julie: 'Pearl's Place'*	Damien Glenn Caroline John S. Casey Julie Tracey	 ✓ ✓	*1* *1* *2* *obs.* *3* *3* *1*	 ✓ ✓
Tuesday Introductory Activity: *Children from Group I tell story of 'Jack & the Beanstalk'. Show how they prepared for it. Discuss.* Silent Reading Responding to Reading: *Conference Group: 'The One in the Middle is the Green Kangaroo', by J. Blume → Dianne, Lucy, Barlowe, Rebecca, Peter.* 2. *Chart drawn up for Giants. List words & phrases & classify under headings:* *Giant Faces	What they Wear	What they do* Share Time: *Katie: Read selection of poems 'Shel Silverstein'.*	Keith Martin Liam Lucy Bradley Barlowe Malcolm	 ✓ ✓ ✓ ✓ ✓	*2* *3* *1* *1* *2* *1* *2*	✓ ✓

	Name	Conf.	Tchg.Grp	Share T.
Wednesday Introductory Activity: *Read: 'The Selfish Giant' by Oscar Wilde. Draw contrasts between giants read about so far – draw generalisations.* Silent Reading Responding to Reading: *Individual Conference:* *Malcolm – 'Dinosaurs'* *3. Story Ladder → Listing main points from 'The Selfish Giant' → children complete Compare with a partner.* Share Time: *Malcolm: – model of dinosaurs (activity)* *Belinda: – 'The Tales of Mrs. Moppity' – B. Potter.*	Katie		2	✔
	George		3	
	Dianne	✔	2	
	Stacie		3	
	Rhaun		3	
	Jane	✔	3	
	Christine		1	
Thursday Introductory Activity: *Drama: Read 'The Giant & The Cobbler.' children break up into groups & prepare play. (10 mins) Return & perform. (Teacher have cue cards for children to join in reading).* Silent Reading Responding to Reading: *Conferences (individual)* *Caroline: 'The Dead Letter Box' by Jan Mark* *Bradley: 'Up in the Sky'* Share Time: *caroline: 'The Dead Letter Box' activity.*	Timmy		1	✔
	James		3	
	Sasha		3	✔
	Peter	✔	3	
	John-P.		1	
	Michelle		3	
	Susan		2	
	Rebecca	✔	2	

3   Work Plan for Year 5

This Year 5 teacher planned in 4-week blocks. On four days, the children chose their own activities related to the books they were reading. On one day each week, every child had to complete activities set by the teacher.

The 4-week block gave the teacher the overall plan for that time. A separate sheet for each week was also kept, as this not only gave planning details, but provided space for record keeping as well. As a result, continuous record keeping was built into the program, and provided a valuable base for evaluation. This weekly sheet recorded which children participated in individual conferences, group conferences and share time. As the week progressed, a glance at the sheet quickly told the teacher which children had participated and which children still had to participate.

The following pages show the planning for three different 4-week blocks. In the second example, it can be seen that the whole class spent some time during two weeks of the block reading *The Sea People* and completing a related assignment and activities. As can be seen in the detailed sample for one week in the third block, the set activities sometimes related to literature being shared with the whole class during the introductory activity. They sometimes required one or two groups to work more closely with a particular title that was available in multiple copies.

Groups need not be set. They will change after each 4-week block and certainly according to purpose.

4 Week Plans   Group Activities — teacher initiated

	GROUP 1	GROUP 2	GROUP 3	GROUP 4
Week 1	*Literature group* "Taylors Troubles" by L. Tarling — introduce book — predicting from title — organize how book will be dealt with in group — begin reading	*Literature group* "The Iron Man" by Ted Hughes — introduce book — read chapter 1 and list important points under chapter heading. Discuss — same format to end of chapter 3	*Author/illustrator* Judith Crabtree — Background to author — Read: "Sparrow Story at the King's Command" — Conference	*Directed reading thinking activity* "A Great Way to Start the Holidays" — challenge — discuss title — predict — read — Do you still think the same? If not, why not? Evidence in text
Week 2	Reading	— Continue reading and discuss important points for each chapter — justify using text	Read: "Legs" and "Carolyn Two" by J. Crabtree — Conference — compare three books by author — Write letter to author	Skimming for detail — use literature books — locate words that describe a character — that express a feeling, etc.
Week 3	Set Reading Task — required written comments — discuss possible activities	— Complete book — Group Conference	Directed reading Thinking activity "A Great Way to Start the Holidays" (Challenge) (as for Group 4)	Author/illustrator Judith Crabtree (as for Group 3) "Sparrow Story at the King's Command"
Week 4	Group Conference — share book with class	Activities — Group — Word Building — words to describe Iron Man Chart — Individual — free choice in responding to story	Skimming for detail (as for Group 4)	"Legs" and "Carolyn Two"

Group Activities — teacher initiated

	GROUP 1	GROUP 2	GROUP 3	GROUP 4
Week 1	Author: Michael Rosen — "Quick Let's Get Out of Here!" — background Read: — Going Through Old Photos — Conference	Using a thesaurus — revise — activity sheet	As for Group 1	Y.A. "The Earthquake Cake" — read ➤ Directed reading-thinking-activity. — predict, read, justify, etc. — discuss
Week 2	Read: — "Chocolate Cake" — "Harry and The Gerbils" — "Washing Up Time" Conference: — Follow Up Activity ➤ children write own story in similar style.	*Group* — example of text given — replace underlined words *Individual* — Use own literature books ➤ find new words using thesaurus. What happens to text?	As for Group 1	— working in pairs discuss text ➤ use conference sheet questions for guide. — meet as whole group and discuss responses.
Weeks 3 & 4	Whole Class Literature *The Sea People* by Müller & Steiner — introduce — read/discuss/re-read — focus on illustrations; strong authors' message; effects of greed, etc. — literature assignment — related activities — sharing together — related literature			

Group Activities — teacher initiated

	GROUP 1	GROUP 2	GROUP 3	GROUP 4
W e e k 1	*Poetry* Banjo Paterson — background to author Time line of his life. Relate his poetry to events in his life. Read "Lost" and discuss.		Poetry "With My Swag All On My Shoulder" Anon. Co-operative cloze	
W e e k 2	Listening to tape "Clancy of the Overflow" "Man from Iron-bark" — choral reading — vocab used — relate to timeline — comparisons	*Literature Group* "Two Village Dinosaurs" by P. Arkle Introduce — discuss — read — predict, etc.	Banjo Paterson — background — time line (as for Group 1), but read "Reverend Mullineaux" and discuss	*Literature group* "Tales of a Fourth Grade Nothing" by J. Blume Introduce — read
W e e k 3	"Man from Snowy River" — focus/poets intentions/char-acters/style, etc. — wall mural		"Clancy of the Overflow" and "Man from Ironbark" (as for Group 1) but singing	
W e e k 4	"With My Swag All On My Shoulder" Anon. — compare with Banjo's style, theme, focus,etc. — co-operative cloze	*Group Conference* *Activities*	"Mulga Bill's Bicycle" —focus, rhythm, main characters, etc. — relate to time line — wall story	*Group Conference* *Activities*

Provide opportunity for Groups 1 and 3 to share together

Next page shows details for one week from this 4-week block

(This weekly plan details one week of the 4 week plan as shown on preceding page).

Language Workshop — focus on Reading
Week Ending:

Focus for Introductory Activity: *Storytelling*	Name	Conf.	Tchg. Grp	Share T.
Monday Introductory Activity: *Tell children the story of 'The Little Match Girl.' What made it a good story to tell?* Silent Reading Responding to Reading *Group 1: Poetry: Banjo Paterson. Discuss background. Time line of major events in his life. Read 'Lost'—discuss focus, authors intentions etc. Record Poems on time line.* *Group 4: Lit group: 'Tales of a 4th Grade Nothing'— J. Blume, introduce - Read (Chpt. 1-3) independently.* Share Time: *Deanne: Activity — A Taste of Blackberries* *sasha: Rebecca at Sunnybrook Farm.*	Paul Dean W Marnie Krish Justin Brendan Jackie Deanne	✓ ✓ ✓ ✓	✓ ✓ ✓	 ✓ ✓ ✓
Tuesday Introductory Activity: *Discuss importance of eye contact, voice changes etc. in telling stories. Practice with a friend in pairs → use intro of a well known fairy tale.* Silent Reading: Responding to Reading: *Group 2: Lit group: 'Two Village Dinosaurs'— P. Arkle: Reading, predicting, justifying using text.* *Group 3: Poetry: 'With My Swag All On My Shoulder'—Anon. Read/Discuss. Co-operative justify choice of words/reach consensus.* Share Time: *Christine: 'Superfudge'— J. Blume.* *→ Author's intentions/read favourite part etc.*	Amber Dean R. Glenn Ashley George David Leeanne Maree	 ✓ ✓ ✓ ✓	✓ ✓ ✓ ✓	

	Name	Conf.	Tchg. Grp	Share T.
Wednesday Introductory Activity: *Split class in two →* *Tell ½ the class an aboriginal legend - They* *listen carefully then retell it to children who were* *outside → discuss success of this.* Silent Reading:	Tabitha		✓	
	Tanya			
	Sasha			✓
Responding to Reading: *Group Conferences:* *'Helen Keller' - Christine/Trudi.* *'Herman the Great' - George, Justin, Glenn, David.* *Individual Conferences:* *'Riddle of The Trumpalar Tree' - Dean W.* Share Time:	Christine	✓	✓	✓
	Brendan		✓	
	Kaine		✓	
Dean W: 'Queen of The Wheat Castles' - C. Mattingley. *Jackie H: 'When the Wind Blows' - R. Briggs - Activity.*	Kylie		✓	
Thursday Introductory Activity: *Swap groups over.* *Tell children 'Beowulf The Warrior' to ½ class.* *Let them listen then retell it to other children →* *discuss how it went.*	Michelle			
	Trudi	✓		
Silent Reading:	Rebecca		✓	
Responding to Reading: *Individual Conferences:* *Leeanne C. — 'Playing Beatie Bow' - R. Park* *Jackie H. — 'When The Wind Blows' - R. Briggs* *Paul D. — 'In the Garden Bad Things' -* *D. McCleod.*	Matthew		✓	
	Brett		✓	
Share Time: *David - 'Fantastic Mr. Fox' - R. Dahl*				

References

Fleet, A., & Martin, L., *Thinking it Through*, Nelson, 1985.

Turbill, J. & Butler, A., *Towards a Reading/ Writing Classroom*, Primary English Teaching Association, 1984.

5 INTRODUCTORY ACTIVITIES

Purpose of the Introductory Activities

The beginning of each reading session provides the teacher with an opportunity to open the world of literature to children and to broaden their experiences within it.

This first part of the session when all are together allows the teacher, with the children, to build up the 'reading community' which is so necessary to support the development of children's reading abilities and attitudes.

Because this part of the session is teacher-initiated, it also allows the teacher to introduce books and authors, to show and discuss the work of different illustrators, to introduce various forms of literature, and so on. The examples given in this chapter show how the introductory activity allows the teacher to integrate reading with the other areas of language and with other curriculum areas. By intergrating with the curriculum in this way, the teacher helps the children to clarify ideas, develop concepts, explore approaches to different kinds of literature, and compare different responses to literature. Using curriculum areas such as drama and art/craft to express understandings of what has been read, helps the children talk and learn from and about each other.

A major aim of the introductory activity is to help children know what to look for, and what to ask, when they are involved in their *own* reading and writing.

If the teacher asks a question such as, 'Why do you think the author may have written this book?' the children may ask the same question when they are reading on their own. Armed with many such questions, they are able to draw more from their reading material.

The focus is great. I like listening to other people's stories that they've written and talking about them. They make you want to write your own stories.

Rebecca

Typical questions might include:

- What does the author have to say?
- Is the author saying it clearly?
- Does the author provide enough information?
- How do the illustrations support the message?
- How are these books similar/different?
- Why do you think the author chose to write in this form?

Ideas for Planning

Sometimes, unplanned and spontaneous introductory activities occur, and these should be grasped and used to advantage whenever possible. However, the introduction to each reading session is very important, and planning should always be purposeful.

Planning can be guided by having a **focus** for a week or any other appropriate length of time. Often, this focus links both reading and writing. Through any weekly focus, all areas of language can be attended to:

- listening
- speaking
- reading
- writing
- thinking

"FOCUS FOR THE WEEK... GRANDPARENTS"

Ideas for a focus are numerous:
- a particular author and his or her work
- a particular illustrator
- an author/illustrator
- content; common themes; links
- books with similar characters
- series; sequels
- poetry; chants; rhymes
- words of songs
- genres; forms; styles
- fiction/non-fiction
- nursery rhymes; fairy stories
- myths; legends; folk tales
- biography; autobiography
- moods (humorous stories; sad stories; mysterious stories)
- story settings; role of author and/or illustrator
- storyline development

Obviously, during this teacher-directed introductory session, much valuable teaching about literature will occur. The introductory session could be used to celebrate, or share enjoyment of, literature, or to help children with any common difficulties.

Jonathan Jo has a mouth
like an O
And a wheelbarrow
full of surprises
If you ask for a bat
or something like that
He's got it whatever
the size is.

Penny

RETOLD WITH PICTURES
by
Mary Anne Brown

Doctor
in a shower of

Cinderella

Hansel & Gretel

RETOLD BY

Humpty Dumpty

Humpty Dumpty sat on
the wall
Humpty Dumpty had a
great fall
All the king's horses and
All the king's men
Couldn't put Humpty together
again

Two, four, six,
eight
Mary at the
cottage gate
Eating cherries
off a plate
Two, four, six
eight.

Why the
Echidna has
its spines..

Once upon a time
when the earth was
only a big desert...

ALEXANDER BEETLE

I had a little beetle And beetle was

his name. I called him Alex-

Introductory Activities from one Year 5 Classroom

The focuses taken from one Year 5 program for 10 weeks were:

Henry Lawson,
- short story ('The Loaded Dog')
- poems ('The Old Bark School', 'Ballad of the Drover')
- content related to Social Studies unit on early Australia   2 weeks

Informational Books,
- *The First Fleet*
- *Eureka Stockade*
- *Crossing the Blue Mountains* (illus. Roland Harvey)
- continuing the Social Studies unit   2 weeks

Miming and role playing favourite characters   1 week

Shel Silverstein's poetry,
- 'Warning'
- 'Bandaids'
- 'True Story'   1 week

Rhonda and David Armitage,
- authors/illustrators
- *The Lighthouse Keeper's Lunch*
- *Icecreams for Rosie*
- links between text and illustrations, implications for writing program   1 week

Whole class conferencing
- how to discuss a book: how to prepare for a conference   1 week

'Naughty Children' theme
- *Tale of Mucky Mabel* and *Tale of Georgie Grubb* by Jeanne Willis
- *Dreadful David* by Sally Odgers   1 week

Writing 'Required Comments'
- share *A Dark Dark Tale* by Ruth Brown: class contributions to written comments.
- share Danish folktale *A Stork is Not Always a Stork:* class written comments.
- share poems from *Hailstones and Halibut Bones* by Mary O'Neill: class written comments.   1 week

Several examples of planned focuses follow here. Other suitable introductory activities are included in the companion volume to this book, *Write On: A Conference Approach to Writing* (1985). The one whole-class activity can serve as an introduction for both the writing and reading sessions.

Detailed Examples of Introductory Activities

1 Focus: *Author* **Chris Van Allsburg**
(Suitable for Years 5 and 6)

Picture-story books by Chris Van Allsburg provide an excellent focus for older children.

Read: *Jumanji*
    The Wreck of the Zephyr
    In the Garden of Abdul Gasazi

Contrasts between the author's style of writing, illustrations, intentions for writing the books, and so on, are easily drawn. All the books provide a subtle twist in their endings which provoke much discussion.

Examples of questions might be:
• Why do you think Chris Van Allsburg wrote the books?
• How do the illustrations reflect the story lines?
• Why did he illustrate in colour in "The Wreck of the Zephyr" but in black and white in the other titles?
• In what ways are the characters similar/different?

If this author and his work are used for the focus over a week, a possible plan could be:

Mon   Introduce author/illustrator — biographical information. Show the three books. Have children predict from the titles and other information on the front covers what they think the books will be about. Read *Jumanji*. Discuss ideas, author's intentions, illustrations, ending.

Tues   Read *The Wreck of the Zephyr*. Discuss (as above).

Wed   Read *In the Garden of Abdul Gasazi*. Discuss (as above).

Thur   Compare and contrast all three books. Words to describe main characters — list under headings.

Fri   Discuss particular points — introductions, endings, illustrations, and so on. Encourage children's personal responses.

2 Focus: Books having the common theme of **'Old Age'**

(Suitable for Years 4, 5, 6)

This particular theme allows children to draw upon their own experiences to express their beliefs about old age and the expectations they have of older people. It also allows relationships between younger people and older people to be considered. This theme can be further developed by, or integrated with, social studies.

Each day, one book may be read and discussed, with the children comparing its ideas about older people with their own knowledge and experience.

A wide variety of literature is available for this theme.

Examples:

Base, Graeme, *My Grandma Lived in Gooligulch*
Baker, Jeannie, *Grandmother*
Rylant, Cynthia, *Miss Maggie*
Miles, M., *Annie and the Old One*
Broome, E. & Dyer, T., *Wrinkles*
Moore, J., *Granny Stickleback*
Newman, N., *My Granny Was a Frightful Bore (But She Isn't Any More)*
Bartoli, J., *Nonna*
Wilson, F., *Super Gran*

One teacher's approach:

The titles were shared over a three-week period. A chart was drawn up so that, as each title was discussed, summaries of main points could be recorded. As the content of this chart grew, it was constantly referred to during discussion time for comparison purposes. Lists of words used to describe grandmothers and the younger characters were also compiled, and were useful in helping define the various characters, relationships between young and old, and parallel characters in different titles.

Some examples of comparison:

- The style of writing and the illustrations in *My Grandma Lived in Gooligulch* were compared with the style of writing and illustrations in *My Granny Was a Frightful Bore (But She Isn't Any More)* and *Wrinkles*.
- Grandmas behaving in inappropriate ways;
- The close relationship that can develop between grandmas and children, as in *Annie and The Old One* and *Grandmother;*
- The use of collage to illustrate *Grandmother* was compared with the ways in which the other books were illustrated.

Obviously, the direction that such a theme takes is dependent upon the individual responses of a particular class of children.

However, some final questions that could be considered include:

- What are the author's intentions?
- What have we learned about old age that we didn't know before?
- Which books remind us most about ourselves and our own grandmothers?
- How do different people cope with growing old?
- How can our 'stereotypes' about old people be misleading?

3 Focus: A. B. (Banjo) Paterson
(Suitable for Years 5 and 6)

Banjo Paterson's poems have a strong story line and reflect a humour that children can enjoy.

This focus was used as an introductory activity over a two-week period to tie in with a social studies unit on 'early Australia'. As a result of the work which had already been done in social studies, a Time Line showing the major events in Paterson's life was drawn up.

Two poems, 'The Man from Ironbark' and 'Clancy of the Overflow', were considered in detail, while others were briefly referred to.

Week 1:
Entries were made on the Time Line to show when the two poems were written. Events in Paterson's life at the time were seen to influence the poems.

The teacher read 'The Man From Ironbark' and discussions centred on the mood and style of writing. The children listened to a tape of the song 'The Man From Ironbark' and learned to sing it themselves.

Groups of children practised choral reading of different verses of the poem and then 'performed' the whole poem as a class activity.

Week 2:
The teacher read 'Clancy of the Overflow' to the children and there was much discussion of what life was like at the time.

Follow-up readings were used to discuss Paterson's use of words and the rhythm and pace of his language.

Again, the children practised choral reading of verses and 'performed' the whole poem as a class activity.

The two poems were compared, with similarities being drawn and contrasts being made with respect to the 'pictures' described by the poems, character description, setting and story line.

4 Focus: 'Windy Weather'

An introductory activity for Prep/1.

Literature:

Pat Hutchins, *The Wind Blew* (Picture Puffins, 1978)

Anita Hewett, *Mrs Mopple's Washing Line* (Picture Puffins, 1970)

Any 'wind' poems *(The Arbuthnot Anthology of Children's Literature*, Scott, Foresman & Co., 1976, is a particularly useful source.)

The Wind Blew

Start with brief discussion about windy weather:

- Do you like windy days?
- What can happen if the wind is too strong?
- When do we like it to be windy?

Introduce the book to the children and read it with expression and rhythm (you need to practise beforehand!)

Discussion:

Listen and respond to the children's first reactions.

If it seems appropriate

- ask the children if they have had any similar experiences
- ask why they thought Pat Hutchins wrote the story
- ask if they liked the ending.

How do the illustrations show that it's windy?

Read again:

This time, encourage the children to read along with you. The natural rhyme and rhythm will aid this.

Activities:

If the book is a popular one, have a group of children illustrate pages so that you can write enlarged text into a Big Book format. The text in this Big Book could be changed to include members of the class as characters.

Select from these activities if appropriate. Encourage children's responses through their own activities.

- Make mobiles of everything that blew away; label the objects.
- Create a wall story (group writing) about children's own experiences of windy weather; this could be reproduced as small, individual books.
- List rhyming words on chart (opportunities for incidental word study, but don't over-do it!).

Focus time is good because we compare our ideas together and learn more about authors and illustrators.

Christine

Mrs Mopple's Washing Line

Before reading, prepare material or paper cut-outs of: a frilly pink petticoat, a pair of woolly bedsocks, two white gloves and a red spotted handkerchief. Hang these (in order) on a line. Cardboard cut-outs of the animals could also be made (or it might be easier to use pictures).

Read the story. Children *may* just listen the first time, but will certainly want to join in during subsequent readings. The clothes on the line and the animal pictures or cut-outs will help children remember the cumulative verse.

Encourage discussion. If appropriate, ask questions such as:
- Why did Mrs Mopple want the wind to blow at the beginning of the story?
- How do you think the animals felt?
- Have you ever had trouble with your washing at home?

Activities:
Provide all the repeated phrases (such as 'A pig in a petticoat') and ask the children to sequence them. The phrases could be written on cardboard strips. If each phrase is written on the bottom of a sheet and reproduced, the children could order the pages, illustrate them and have their own copies of the 'refrain' for reading material. Illustrations could be done with material collage. Innovations on text: keep same sentence structure but change the items of clothing and the animals. Write up on a wall chart.

Poetry

There are many suitable poems about wind and weather which should be read and enjoyed. Favourite ones could be written on charts or learned for choral presentation. Heed Moira Robinson's warnings about 'How Not To "Teach" Poetry'. (In McVitty, W. ed., *Word Magic: poetry as a shared adventure*, Primary English Teaching Association, 1985)

'Linking the Literature'

Which story or poem did you like best? Why? What problems did the characters have in the two stories? Wind is sometimes a nuisance.

- When is it a danger?
- When is it a friend?

Are there any special words that sound like the wind? Any words that make the wind sound strong?

Ask the librarian if there are any other stories or poems about wind.

5 Focus: *Meg and Mog* Books

A selection of books from the *Meg and Mog* series by Helen Nicoll and Jan Pienkowski can be used as an introduction to serial reading for young children, as each book has the same main characters. One or two titles could be read during each introductory session, and ideas covering other areas of the curriculum are suggested here.

Teacher Preparation

- Life-size cut-outs of the main characters, with names, to be displayed in classroom prior to reading books.
- Collect appropriate poems about witches.
- Collect other picture-story books about witches.

Activities planned for the first title in the series, *Meg and Mog*, are suggested below. This example could follow the alternative session plan suggested for the Prep-1 years in chapter 4 (see page 26):

Introductory, whole-class activity ⎫
Responding (individual and ⎬ 'Meg and Mog'
group activities) ⎭

Silent Reading ⎫ self-selected materials
Share Time ⎭

Activities

- Introduce the cut-out characters. Invite comments about books the children have read about witches.
- Read *Meg and Mog* to class. (Be dramatic, and enthusiastic!)
- Allow time for oral response.
- Talk about spells; list ingredients used in Meg's spell.

- Children (individuals or groups) could write their own spells and write them on cardboard cut-outs of cauldrons.
Brainstorm a list for spells: to make you fatter; to make you disappear; to make you cry.
- If story is well-liked, make a 'Big Book' with the children and use for procedures common to shared-book experience.
- Re-read story, drawing attention to the 'sound effect' words. List these words (make them graphically appealing, as in text). Children join in and read these 'sound words' with teacher.

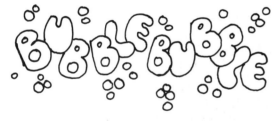

- Discuss the way other words have been written in the text (different colours; different shapes and sizes). How do these make you feel?
- Make masks of main characters for drama activities. Use instruments for sound effects.

More Suggestions for Introductory Activities

The following is a 'pot-pourri' of ideas that could be considered by teachers who want to plan their introductory activities around an author or author/illustrator, or around a topic or theme. Obviously, the list is not exhaustive, but it can give teachers a good start. There are many references that teachers should consult when they need new authors, illustrators or topics for introductory activities.

The examples below have been selected with teachers of Prep to Year 3 in mind. However, any of them could be used with older children, depending on the teacher's purpose. The purpose could be sheer enjoyment and fun; it could be to consider the interplay between text and illustrations; it could be to develop understanding of publishing techniques that would help the children with the publishing of their own writing.

Authors and/or Illustrators

Janet & Allan Ahlberg, *Burglar Bill*
Peepo!
Funny Bones

Pamela Allen, *Berti and the Bear*
Who Sank the Boat?
Mr Archimedes Bath

Jeannie Baker, *Grandmother*
Grandfather
Millicent
Home in the Sky

Peggy Blakey, *Firework Party*
Oscar on the Moon
Rain
The Smallest Christmas Tree

Ruth Brown, *If At First You Do Not See*
Crazy Charlie
A Dark, Dark Tale

Eric Carle, *The Very Hungry Caterpillar*
The Bad-tempered Ladybird
Watch Out! A Giant!
   (Also illustrated *Brown Bear Brown Bear*
What Do You See? by Bill Martin Jnr)

Donald Crews, *Carousel*
Freight Train
Truck

Mem Fox, *Possum Magic*
Wilfred Gordon McDonald Partridge

Mirra Ginsburg, *Across the Stream*
Good Morning Chick
The Strongest One of All
Two Greedy Bears

Pat Hutchins, *Rosie's Walk*
The Wind Blew
One-Eyed Jake
Don't Forget the Bacon!
Goodnight Owl!
Titch
The Tale of Thomas Mead

Ezra Jack Keats, *Louie*
The Snowy Day
Whistle for Willie
Maggie and the Pirate
A Letter to Amy
Peter's Chair
The Trip

Steven Kellog, *Can I Keep Him?*
The Mysterious Tadpole
Pinkerton, Behave!
The Island of the Skog

Judith Kerr, *The Tiger Who Came to Tea*
Mog and the Baby
Mog, the Forgetful Cat
Mog's Christmas

Leo Lionni, *Fish Is Fish*
Swimmy
Frederick
Geraldine the Music Mouse
Little Blue and Little Yellow

David McKee, *Elmer*
Not Now, Bernard
The Hill and the Rock

Beatrix Potter, *Tale of Peter Rabbit*
Tale of Floppsy Bunnies
Tale of Mr Jeremy Fisher
Tale of Jemima Puddle-Duck

Peter Spier, *Bored — Nothing To Do*
Nothing Like a Fresh Coat of Paint
Rain

Brian Wildsmith, *Daisy*
Seasons
Trunk
The Miller, the Boy and the Donkey

Lorraine Wilson, *Footy Kids series*
Country Kids series
City Kids series

Topics or Themes

Animals/Pets
Norman Bridwell, *Clifford* books
Mike Dickinson, *My Brothers Silly*
Eric Hill, *Where's Spot?* (and sequels)
Robert Lopshire, *Put Me in the Zoo*
Sarah McLeish, *Rambo the Champion*
Margaret Mahy, *A Lion in the Meadow*

Crocodiles
Aliki, *Keep Your Mouth Closed Dear*
Ruth Brown, *Crazy Charlie*
Roald Dahl, *The Enormous Crocodile*
David McPhail, *Alligators are awful (and they
          have terrible manners too)*

Family
Margo Blaine, *The Terrible Thing that Hap-
          pened at Our House*
Mary Cockett, *The Birthday*
Babette Cole, *The Trouble With Mum*
Elleanor Schick, *Home Alone*
Bernadette Watts, *David's Waiting Day*
Betty Yurdin, *The Tiger in the Teapot*

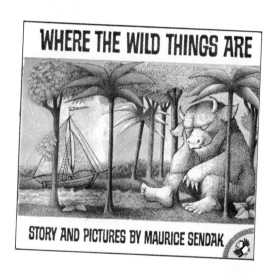

Fantasy
Colin Hawkins, *Snap, Snap*
Maurice Sendak, *Where the Wild Things Are*
Margaret Mahy, *The Dragon of an Ordinary
          Family*

Fear
Margaret Kubelka, *Abracadabra!*
Jill Murphy, *On the Way Home*
James Stevenson, *What's Under My Bed*
Bernard Vaber, *Goodnight Ben*
Jeanne Willis, *Tale of Fearsome Fritz*

Friendship
E. J. Keats, *Louis*
Kim Lardner, *The Sad Little Monster and the
          Jelly Bean Queen*
Jenny Wagner, *John Brown Rose and the Mid-
          night Cat*
Lynd Ward, *The Biggest Bear*
Brian Wildsmith, *Friendship*

Humour

Judi Barrett, *Animals Should Definitely Not Wear Clothing*
Ann Coleridge, *The Friends of Emily Culpepper*
Hazel Edwards, *There's A Hippopotamus on our Roof Eating Cake*
Phyllis Kraslovsky, *The Cow Who Fell in the Canal*
The Man Who Didn't Wash his Dishes
Ruth Park, *When the Wind Changed*
Kathleen Stevens, *The Beast in the Bathtub*

Naughty Children

Jack Gantos, *Rotten Ralph*
Worse Than Rotten Ralph
Terry Ingleby, *Messy Malcolm*
Sally Odgers, *Dreadful David*
Judith Vigna, *The Little Boy Who Loved Dirt and Almost Became a Super Slob*
Elfrida Vipont, *The Elephant and the Bad Baby*
Jeannie Willis, *Tale of Georgie Grubb*
Tale of Mucky Mabel

The Sea

Rhonda & David Armitage, *The Lighthouse Keeper's Lunch*
Icecreams for Rosie
E. J. Keats, *Maggie and the Pirate*
Leo Lionni, *Fish is Fish*
Colin Thiele, *Storm Boy* (picture story book)
Margaret Wild, *There's a Sea in my Bedroom*

Witches

Sue Alexander, *Witch, Goblin and Sometimes Ghost*
Mary Barry, *Simon and the Witch*
Bruce Degan, *The Little Witch and the Riddle*
John Moore, *Granny Stickleback*
Helen Nicoll, *Meg and Mog* books
Pat Traynor, *The Would-be Witch of Williamstown*

Picture Story Books are **not** just for infants! Upper school children love many of the picture story books enjoyed by younger children. For example, books by Ezra Jack Keats have wide appeal and the issues he explores through picture story books can be discussed at various levels of sophistication. In addition, many picture story books are now being written specifically for older children. Some examples are:

Müller, J. & Steiner, J., *The Sea People,*

Steiner, J., *Rabbit Island,*

Briggs, R., *The Tin-Pot Foreign General and the Old Iron Woman,* Hamish Hamilton, 1984.

Note: These titles were sampled from the catalogue of a primary school library. Most libraries have books like these which should be used as an essential part of the school's reading program. In fact, the library should be the main reading scheme in every school!

References

Allen, Roach Van, *Language Experiences in Communication,* Houghton Mifflin Co., 1976.

Bailes, J. (ed) *The Reading Bug and How to Catch It,* Ashton Scholastic, 1980.

Dalton, J., *Adventures in Thinking,* Nelson, 1985.

Johnson, T. & Louis, D., *Literacy Through Literature,* Methuen, 1985.

Martin, Bill, Jnr., *Sounds of Language series,* Holt Rinehart and Winston, 1970.

Parry, J. & Hornsby, D., *Write On: A Conference Appoach to Writing,* Martin Educational, 1985.

Introduction

Reading is not a passive activity. The reader must reconstruct the author's meaning and can only do this by relating what they are reading to their own knowledge, experience and emotions. This reconstruction develops and changes as new information is acquired from the text. If there are no transactions between the reader's personal knowledge, experience and emotions and the author's intended meaning, the reader is merely pronouncing words or 'barking at print'. This is true at all stages of reading, including the very earliest.

The strength or quality of the transactions that occur between the author and the reader provides a measure of the success of the material. C. S. Lewis has argued that it is the *quality of response* which differentiates literary readers from non-literary readers.

Children's Responses

When we know how children respond to literature, our planning is much more appropriate. Studying their responses (particularly during the conference) helps us to plan because we learn more about the different kinds of literature that should be provided, more about the kinds of questions that should be asked, more about the children themselves and more about the kinds of activities that will help to encourage growth in response.

Since reading is an active process and influenced by the reader's own knowledge, experience and emotions, responses have a subjective element. It is impossible to respond to reading material as if the text 'exists in its own autonomous world independently of both reader and author' (Rosen, quoted by Grant, 1984). What children read cannot be separated from their own experiences of life.

'The attempt to disconnect our experience of literature from the rest of our life experiences constitutes a travesty of what literature offers, as well as a misunderstanding of the nature of the learning and language processes.' (Grant, 1984, p.3)

Reading programs cannot be dictated by the books in a scheme. If anything, the library should be seen as the indispensible 'reading scheme' and should continue to be the place where children may borrow self-chosen books of all kinds. This opportunity should be built into their daily reading program and have priority over getting through levels in a scheme.

Effects of Life Experiences on Response

Children's life experiences have a major influence on the books they choose to read and how they respond to those books. Words stir up different thoughts and feelings for each reader. If you have just had a beautiful new pool installed and it's a hot summer's day, the word 'pool' will have a very different personal meaning for you than for the reader who has just had his or her back garden devasted by an above-ground pool that collapsed!

Personal meanings may be different from commonly shared or public meanings. Readers select from all their personal thoughts and feelings: they focus on some and leave others at the 'edge of awareness'. Rosenblatt (1983) has described how readers guide this selective process. They set up expectations, or make predictions, and use these to control their selections. They focus on elements which suggest a tentative framework for meaning and this framework reduces the range of further choices as meaning is developed. Expectations and guides for selection are modified if further text does not support the developing framework of meaning. And the predominant influences on this process are the experiences of life. These experiences have a major effect on the books children choose to read and on their responses. However, their life experiences include their classroom experiences!

> The teacher has an important role in providing children with book experiences that will positively influence the children's selections and reading behaviours.

Variations in Response

Since response is a product of the text itself and the experiences of the author and the reader, it includes both subjective *and* objective elements. Children will respond to the same material in different ways, and this has several important implications. Aspects of comprehension will differ for each individual reader. There may be 'right' or 'wrong' answers to literal comprehension questions, but literal comprehension is also limited comprehension. At the inferential, critical and evaluative levels, answers will not be simply right or wrong. Another implication is that teachers must allow diversity of response and provide opportunities for response through discussion, art and craft, cooking, music and movement, drama, games, writing, and various media.

Children also have the option of *not* responding publicly; of not sharing their reading.

> 'Some stories or poems are too special, too personal to be shared. The child may want to savor them, to read them again and again in order to hold their thoughts close to him. A teacher should know the children in the class well enough to know what will help each student have memorable experiences with books.'
> (Huck, 1979, p.641)

Purpose for Reading and Stance Taken

To respond to reading effectively, readers must also decide on their *purpose* for reading. Purpose plays a large part in determining which aspects of the text readers will attend to and which they will ignore; which thoughts and feelings they will focus upon and which ones they will leave at the edge of awareness. Rosenblatt refers to this as the reader's choice of 'stance'. She describes one end of a continuum as the 'efferent stance' where the reader attends to the public meaning to be carried away from the reading. *After* the reading, the reader's intention may be to recall and analyze what he or she has retained. When a reader chooses the 'aesthetic stance', he or she chooses to focus 'primarily on what is being personally lived through, cognitively and affectively, *during* the reading event'. (1985, p.102)

Efferent and aesthetic reading refer to the *reader's choice* of stance and not to the text itself; a reader can choose to read any text in either way. However, much of our reading lies somewhere between the efferent and aesthetic ends of the continuum.

What are we Looking for?

We must allow children to tell or show us what they really think and must avoid the temptation to tell them what to think. We must be very careful not to put preconceived ideas into the children's minds, as we want their genuine response, not the response that they think we want.

We must *listen* to children's responses to books to know how they are thinking and feeling. 'The process of the interpretation is more important than the interpretation itself; both are of greater value than the content of the book or the craft of the writing.' (Huck, 1979, p.738)

To discover how and why children are interpreting text, teachers must listen to them and discuss *their* thoughts and feelings with them. This is why a small group conference is so useful and so important.

> If we know both the child's interpretation and how he or she arrived at it, we have important information.

When teachers have this information, they are able to assist the development of each and every child.

Developing Response to Reading

Elements of developing response have been described in various ways. Some influential authors are James Britton. D. W. Harding and Louise Rosenblatt, who have written extensively.

Rosenblatt was one of the first to describe the transactional nature of reading by maintaining that readers perform or re-create the text into a 'new work'.

Harding has described how important it is for a reader to understand that a book is an author's way of communicating what he or she has to say. The reader must relate not just to the book, but also to the author speaking through the book. Harding has also emphasized that 'It is literature, not literary criticism, that is the subject.' When children's responses to reading draw heavily upon personal experience (when they respond with statements like 'He's just like me!') this should be encouraged. Affective response should never be discouraged by a demand for analysis or objective interpretation. When it is, readers begin to distrust their personal response.

Similarly, Britton has emphasized that we must develop and extend the responses that children are already making — we must not begin with how *we* want the children to respond. Satisfaction, says Britton, must *always* be an outcome of reading. 'Reading without satisfaction is like the desperate attempts we make to keep a car going when it has run out of petrol'. (1977, p.110) Teachers must remember this in their endeavours to help readers respond to reading.

A mature or considered response will include the following:

1 Attending willingly (accepting reading as valuable, interesting or enjoyable)	
2 Elementary perception and comprehension of the scene	Entering into and Responding with; establishes the reader's relationship with the novel. **Dimension 1**
3 Empathising with characters, problems or action	

4 Drawing analogies with life and searching for self-identity (learning and feeling things that help one's own life and self-understanding)	
5 Detached evaluation of the characters and what they do and suffer	Evaluating and Responding to; establishes the reader's relationship with the author. **Dimension 2**
6 Reviewing the whole work as a social convention and accepting or rejecting the author's stated or implied values	

(Adapted from Harding, 1967, and Grant, 1982)

Readers who take the step from the first dimension of 'entering into and responding with' to the second dimension of 'evaluating and responding to' are moving from a relationship with the novel only to a relationship with the novel *and* the author. Grant warns us that less practised readers may fail to take this second step and writes of Harding's belief that this second step is decisive. It is decisive because it indicates that the reader has an awareness that fiction is a social convention and that he or she can view a text as one form of communication used by the author.

A full or considered reponse will include all of the elements listed above, but literature is defined broadly in chapter 2 and elements of response would certainly vary according to the type of literature read.

Elements of Response; Not Stages!

A description of such elements of response should not be used as a list of 'stages' of response. 'Stages' are never found to be a true reflection of what readers do. Stages may seem to have a 'logical coherence', but they are abstractions and have no psychological reality. Stages can also be used inappropriately to direct attention to the product or final outcome of reading and to label a reader at a particular level. However, a reader may be responding at different levels, depending on the material being read. A reader may also be responding at different levels to different aspects of the same piece of literature. **No individual reader is ever simply at one stage.**

An awareness of elements of response may, however, help to form a framework within which teachers may operate. Such awareness may help teachers know what to look for in children's responses; it may help them to interpret what they observe; it may help them determine developmental or directional criteria for children's progress.

Verbal and Non-verbal Response

There are multiple opportunities during the reading session to tune in to children's verbal responses, but **by far the most effective way of harnessing verbal response is to conduct individual or small group conferences.**

Conferences are an essential part of any effective reading program. The role of the teacher, the setting and 'conference climate', the form a conference takes, getting conferences started, conferences with younger children — these and other matters are considered in chapter 7.

Non-verbal responses are observed while children are actually reading and while they are engaged in activities which result from their reading. Chapter 8 looks at how children respond to reading through activities. Chapter 8 also considers the importance of opportunities being made for children to share their responses to books. The sharing at the end of each reading session enables children to combine both verbal and non-verbal response, and is an important part of every reading program.

References

Britton, J., 'Response to Literature' in Meek et al., *The Cool Web,* The Bodley Head, 1977.

Grant, A. N., 'Literacy Response as Story: understanding response in the context of identity' in *English in Australia*, vol. 68, June 1984, pp.3-14.

Grant, A. N., 'Young Readers Reading: a study of personal response to the reading of fiction based on five case studies of students at the upper secondary school level', Doctoral thesis, University of Melbourne, to be published by Routledge & Kegan Paul, 1985.

Harding, D. W., 'Considered Experience: The Invitation of the Novel in English' in *Education*, 1, 2, 1967, pp.7-15.

Huck, C., *Children's Literature in the Elementary School*, 3rd edn. updated, Holt, Rinehart and Winston, 1979.

Rosenblatt, L., 'Viewpoints: Transaction versus interaction — a Terminological Rescue Operation', 19, 1, Feb. 1985, pp.96-107.

7 RESPONDING TO READING 2: THE CONFERENCE

Introduction

The reading conference is the 'guts' of the program.

It is during the conference that many of the important aspects of the reading program are given attention or are influenced by the teacher. It is during the conference that the teacher can more directly influence attitudes, appreciations, understandings, values, actions, behaviour, and so on. But it is also the time when the teacher can come close to children and when the teacher can find out more about the children's interests, reading needs and personal feelings.

The Teacher's Role and Approach

The teacher's attitude and approach to the children in this small group setting are most important. Teachers must love books and must love sharing them with children. If this is not the case, teachers may 'go through the motions', but the conference will *not* be successful.

A poster in one teacher's classroom indicates the positive attitude necessary:

Mr Fisher's TOP OF THE POPS Library choice for [MONDAY]
"Burglar Bill" by Janet and Allan Ahlberg.
"Funniest book I've read in ages" "It's great" Mr Fisher

If you have not discovered children's literature, if you do not choose to read, then you haven't found the right book either! Go back to the end of chapter 2 and find out where to start. When you discover some of the delights waiting for you in books, share your discoveries with the children.

Conference Setting and Climate

The children need to be in a comfortable setting. They may be sitting around a conference table or lying on the carpet. Whatever they are doing, it is most important that each person in the group is able to have eye contact with each of the others (including the teacher) and that a relaxed attitude is fostered. It is important for the teacher to start the session with a concern for physical comfort and relaxed conversation before 'hitting them with the book'.

The children must feel that they are part of the group and that what they have to say will be important and will receive attention. When they are confident that this is so, they will be more willing to share and to take risks. When the climate is open and friendly, embarrassment is avoided and exchange of ideas and feelings is facilitated.

Conference Format

Possible steps for a conference could be:

1 Listen

a Children give their responses to the reading material.

b Response and re-telling provide much information for the teacher about comprehension.

2 Receive, Respond and Discuss

a Let the children lead: RECEIVE what they say and then RESPOND.

b Ask general questions first (about themes, characters, points of view) which you think the children *can* answer.

c Ask more specific or challenging questions next.

d Encourage the children to ask each other questions and to be involved in discussion.

3 Oral Reading for Own Purpose

a to 'prove' a point; to clarify; to check; and so on.

b The purpose of oral reading during a conference is always related to meaning, content, comprehension, or the sheer enjoyment of the language.

4 Planning

a What are you going to do now? (activities/continued reading?)

b What are you going to read next? (related literature/same author/related topic?)

5 Records

May be kept by the teacher and the children at this time (see chapter 12, Record Keeping and Evaluation).

Note: These 'steps' are *not* to be considered as a strait-jacket. Obviously, teachers should be flexible and conduct the conference in a way which will meet the needs of the children.

Getting Conferences Started

Children who have not been used to reading conferences will not at first realize their value. They will not know how a conference can help them. They must learn to prepare for a conference because it is expected that they will eventually come to a conference with a purpose in mind. The purposes vary and may include:

- discussion about something of value/interest to them;
- requests for help with understanding text;
- requests for help with selection of reading material;
- opportunity to share feelings about favourite characters, humorous incidents, special endings, author's use of language;
- desire to hear the viewpoint of others.

> **When conferencing is new to children, the teacher will need to help the children prepare.**

This may be done by requiring them to:

- complete a written comment to bring to the conference;
- draw a picture of the main character or the setting;
- bring a list of important characters;
- bring their books with bookmarks inserted, indicating a part they want to share;
- discuss the appropriateness of chapter headings;
- comment on the use of illustrations;
- bring a list of major events and the settings in which they occurred.

During early group conferences, even when the children have prepared for them, teachers may find themselves doing most of the talking and asking most of the questions. Again, this teacher modelling is most important. It demonstrates to children the kinds of questions which should be asked and, from the ensuing discussion and sharing of ideas, the children come to realize how valuable the conference sessions are.

However, as soon as possible, the **children** must take the initiative during the conference session. They must

- ask questions
- listen to others in the group
- discuss issues
- learn to appreciate different points of view.

Conferences with Younger Children

With younger, dependent readers, the conference is often held *while the reading is taking place* rather than after a group has finished reading. The teacher sits with the children and shares a common title with them or 'confers' with them. This kind of sharing with children has always been a necessary part of procedures such as shared book experience, wall stories, language-experience procedures, and so on. So conferences with younger, dependent readers are 'built-in' to procedures already in common use.

However, children in their first year of school have many picture books (no text), simple caption books, nursery rhyme books or experience books, which they can read independently or with little assistance. With these materials, a conference *after* the reading will be appropriate and a format similar to that outlined above can be used.

The Importance of Teacher Modelling

Teacher modelling is important with *all* children, but it is *essential* to model reading behaviours for young children.

As the teacher sits with a group and reads to or with them, the first priority is enjoyment. 'A book, a person, and shared enjoyment; these are the conditions of success.' (Margaret Meek, 1982, p.9)

Margaret Meek also writes about the importance of teacher modelling. ' . . . teaching and learning, to be successful, must be genuinely shared. In the early stages of helping children to learn anything, the adult has to do a great deal.' (p.12) 'The supporting adult who shows him what a book is and how print works, who helps him to discover reading and expects him to be successful, makes all the difference.' (p.31)

The teacher needs to demonstrate and talk about reading behaviours, including:

- selection of titles
- holding of books correctly
- directional conventions
- starting story where the print starts
- picture and text interplay
- use of different print styles
  (e.g. bold, enlarged, italics, fancy)

Questioning

In the Conference Format outlined above, the first important step was to *listen*. Unless teachers really listen to what children say about the material they have read, they will not be able to respond appropriately.

As a result of listening, part of the second step is to ask questions.

It is good advice when we are told to listen more and question less. However, the right question at the right time can be just what individual children need to get them started — maybe even to 'open the flood gates'! Appropriate questions also help to put them on the right track or to indicate a perspective within which the children can develop further understanding.

Questions to get children started are often called 'opening' questions (Graves, 1984). The specific aim is to provide an impetus to get the children talking.

'Following' questions are aimed to *keep* the children talking. The teacher continues to receive what the children say. As a result, the teacher can affirm the children's responses or help them to reconstruct the author's intended meaning. The teacher can also extend or challenge them just beyond their immediate understanding.

'Process' questions help the children to focus on particular elements of the text while also helping them to keep 'oriented' within the overall meaning. They help children effectively use all reading strategies. (They also help the teacher obtain information that will be used to plan future teaching groups.) 'Process' questions will help children to learn about comparisons and contrasts (signalled by words such as but, however, although, yet) about sequence (signalled by words such as first, second, last, before, after, whilst, then, later) about cause and effect (signalled by words such as if . . . then, because, unless, since, so that) about question and answer patterns (signalled by words such as why? how? when? where?) about different functions or paragraphs in longer discourse (introductory, explanatory, narrative, descriptive, defining, transitional and concluding paragraphs).

These types of questions — 'opening', 'following' and 'process' — are also referred to in the companion volume to this text, *Write On: A Conference Approach to Writing*. They are useful categories to have in mind when running conferences in either reading or writing, but obviously questions can be categorized in many other ways.

Bloom's *Taxonomy of Educational Objectives* (1956) categorized questions according to the level of thought required by the respondent:
1 Memory (literal comprehension)
2 Translation
3 Interpretation
4 Application
5 Analysis
6 Synthesis
7 Evaluation

Huck (1979) has given examples of questions (about various pieces of literature) in each of these categories. These examples provide a useful guide to teachers about the kinds of questions that should be asked.

Questions can also be categorized as convergent or divergent. Convergent questions refer mainly to memory or recall and pursue a 'right' or at least 'best' answer. Divergent or open-ended questions require higher level thinking (such as analysis, synthesis and evaluation) encourage all kinds of possibilities and responses, and develop an open-mindeness and tolerance of differences. Divergent questions also provide for *all* children a challenge and a means of responding in their own way.

Dalton (1985) provides useful models for divergent questioning.

Ownership

The concept of 'ownership', often referred to in the literature about writing, is also relevant when talking about children's responses to reading.

It is very important that children have this sense of 'ownership' of their responses to reading, especially during a conference. Ownership is left with the children when their responses are valued and not put down or ignored. Teachers must show that children's responses are valued even if the responses of others are different. When teachers concentrate on the higher levels of thinking and ask divergent questions, then responses *will* vary. This does not mean that all responses are valid, but it *does* mean that all responses are given due consideration and that children are given opportunities to explain their responses, develop them, change them and speculate.

Different Conferences for Different Purposes

Timetabled Group Conferences

Many teachers like to timetable groups of children who are required to attend a very short conference on a regular basis. For example, if you have 30 children, you may see 6 children each day. Since you know which children you will be seeing on any given day, you can refer to their reading folders *before* the timetabled conference. The main intention of these brief conferences is to maintain regular contact with children, to help children set the direction in which they are going, and to 'keep a finger on the pulse'. In one sense, these timetabled conferences are 'house-keeping' conferences, and they can never take the place of conferences based on need or specific purpose.

During a timetabled conference, children simply need to be asked. 'Where are you up to? . . . Do you need help with anything? . . . Have you and I got our records up to date? . . . What are you doing next?'

For 5 or 6 children, this should take only 3 or 4 minutes.

It is useful to show which children are time-tabled each day in your work program or diary. (See examples in chapters 4 and 12.) The number of children in these groups will vary according to the number of children in your class, the number of reading sessions you take in each week and the time you have available for each session. For example, if Monday's session is a shorter one, then you may see only 3 or 4 children in the timetabled conference; if Tuesday's session is a longer one, then it may be possible to timetable 6 or 7 children.

Needs-based Group Conferences

A conference needs to be arranged when several children have been reading:
- the same title
- different titles by the same author
- different titles, different authors, but same illustrator
- different titles and authors, but same subject or theme
- books which can be categorized within the same genre.

So it is possible to have conferences to consider the same title, a particular author, a particular illustrator, or a common subject theme or interest, 'Common genre' conferences are particularly valuable and help experienced readers to draw together common threads in otherwise diverse reading materials. For example, a group might come together to discuss Oscar Wilde's *The Selfish Giant*, George MacDonald's *The Light Princess*, Anita Lobel's *A Birthday for a Princess* and Jay Williams' *Petronella* and *Everyone Knows What a Dragon Looks Like*, because each of these can be classified as a modern fairy tale. Modern fairy tales have the same form as traditional fairy tales, but unlike the traditional fairy tales, they have an identifiable author — they did not grow through oral retellings over many generations. These, and other points, can be considered during a conference where 'genre' is the focus.

Individual Conferences

Individual conferences, of necessity, last only a few minutes, but they give children the opportunity of close attention from and personal sharing with the teacher. They can be time-

tabled or they can occur 'on demand' and at various times throughout the reading session.

Individual conferences may be required in addition to group conferences. They may be required by the teacher or by the child and for various reasons. They are certainly required when the teacher wants to do a closer evaluation than would be possible in a group conference. Many of the techniques for evaluating a child's reading (see chapter 12) require an individual conference. Also, individual conferences are important for children who do not yet participate fully in a group conference or for inexperienced readers who need help with selection of books and who need occasional injections of enthusiasm to build their confidence.

While individual conferences allow close attention and help to meet children's immediate concerns, they do not allow the very important and powerful interacting that occurs between children in group conferences. The importance of co-operative talk, of creative thinking, of active involvement in small learning groups, is well established. Joan Dalton (1985) rightly argues that they are the skills of the future.

Teacher-required Conferences

Sometimes, teachers will require certain children to attend a conference. For example, children who are not getting to conferences often enough because they are having difficulty choosing reading materials with which they can persevere, often benefit from being required to 'sit in' on a group conference. When these children hear the others in the group sharing their enthusiams for particular titles, they are often drawn into the discussion. Even if their initial comments are something like, 'I didn't like that book' or 'I didn't understand that part', the fact that they have discussed their book experiences with others helps to get them 'out of the rut' and in touch with others' book experiences. Experience shows that few of these children will merely 'sit in' with a group; most will talk freely when given the opportunity to express what they feel. This group encounter will do more to help such children than any command handed down by the teacher. Teachers *must* harness peer influence and use it to help other children.

Children who are stuck on the same author will also be helped, and for the same reasons, if they are required to attend a conference.

A less happy reason for requiring a child's attendance at a conference, but nevertheless a valid reason, is that he or she is disrupting the conference by not working independently at that time. Conferences are important and the teacher and the children in the conference group should not be interrupted unnecessarily.

Conference Transcripts

Readers who study the transcript and, if possible, view the videotape 'Responding to Reading', will notice several important aspects which should be outcomes of all conferences.

These include:

1 A positive attitude by all towards other children's contributions. The children listen to each other in a spirit of co-operation. They accept what others say or help each other towards an articulation of what they have understood.

2 The teacher's questions help to draw out common threads or themes.

3 The children use each other's ideas to develop their own.

4 A high level of comprehension is achieved. Little time is spent in simple recall of story or naming of characters or description of setting. Most of the time is spent in discussing how character is revealed, seeing character from different points of view, describing relationships and expressing personal experiences which help to relate to events in the story.

The comprehension achieved or 'drawn out' during a conference is at a much higher level than the comprehension that would be demonstrated by asking children to write answers to another set of questions from the chalkboard or the purple sheet. *The conference allows children to re-live the story, to 're-read' the text with added pairs of eyes.* During the conference, the children bounce ideas off the teacher and each other, they negotiate the text, they use comments from other readers to extend their comprehension, they use the discussion to formulate new questions. None of this is possible when children are asked to write answers to previously prepared questions. There can be no negotiation, no extension beyond the questions actually asked, no following of intuitions, little risk-taking and certainly no room for a little dreaming.

Written answers can be (and still should be) required, but the limitations of writing answers to pre-set questions must be acknowledged. When written answers to specific comprehension questions are required, then children should be asked to write them *after* attending a conference.

Note: We are talking about expected answers to set comprehension questions here. These differ from the 'Required Comments' that the children are asked to keep in their reading books or reading logs. The 'Required Comments' include a 'gut level' reaction to the book. There may be guiding questions to help children consider issues to comment upon, but there are no set questions requiring expected answers.

A Wizard of Earthsea

This novel was read as part of a literature unit with six competent Year 5 readers at Mill Park Primary School, in Melbourne, and is written up in Chapter 14. It was studied in greater detail than other novels and several conferences were held. The excerpts are from Conference 2, Conference 4 and the final conference, Conference 5.

Reading these transcripts will help you get a 'feeling' for what happens in conferences. You will find it rewarding to persevere. The excerpts have been abridged to make the written transcription easier to read.

Excerpts from Conference 2	**Comments**
Conference 2 began with a discussion which reflected on chapter 1 and looked at the developments in chapters 2 and 3. The 'main points' that the children had jotted down were compared and the children had either to justify their points by referring to the text for support, or modify them.	
Teacher What's the author doing in the initial chapters of the book?	Opening question.
Brenton She's just getting us into Earthsea and explaining things. Like, she explains the stuff about the Great House and the characters.	Brenton and Dean are showing that they understand that early chapters have to introduce characters and 'set the scene'.
Dean R She's getting Ged ready for all the adventures he's going to have.	
Tabitha I'm getting used to the words and when I don't know how to say them, I skip over them quickly. I know what they mean but I can't say them. I just say them in my mind. Some are hard to say.	Tabitha has a healthy attitude to the words she's not sure about (particularly the unusual names of some of the characters and places).
Brenton In the third chapter, Ged got humiliated by Jasper because Jasper and Vetch showed tricks that they could do. Then Ged worked secretly on charms to beat Jasper.	
Dean R Ged got mad with Jasper because he showed off his tricks in front of the Lord's wife.	The children have grasped already a key understanding about Ged's behaviour (and of human nature in general).
Sasha Yeah — Ged got extra lessons from the Mage so that he could get back at Jasper.	
Tabitha I want to read that part when he says the spell — it gives me the horrors! *(After asking the children to 'hang on', she finds the part and reads it aloud.)*	Tabitha is responding to a particular part of the text, not only because of its message, but also because of Le Guin's use of language.

Excerpts from Conference 2	**Comments**
Teacher Who do you think are the strong characters?	
Dean R I think Jasper and Ged are a bit like me and Buzz because Buzz is always trying to get the better of me.	Dean is showing that he understands why Ged was jealous.
Brenton (Buzz) What do you mean by that?	
Dean R You do — like, sometimes we're doing something like writing together. You write something good and then I feel like writing something really good.	Both Dean and Brenton relate the book to this aspect of their own lives.
Brenton Yeah. There's a sort of competition between us. Ged and Jasper were competing with each other too I guess.	
Teacher Is that a good thing?	
Brenton Well . . . not if it makes us fight. But we help each other with ideas too.	
Tabitha I loved the part when Ged was reading one of Ogion's books. When he read a spell . . . *(Tabitha searches for text).*	Tabitha responds to a particular part of the text again.
Sasha It's on page 34.	Co-operation from Sasha.
Tabitha *(Reads section.)* It gives me the horrors because in the first part of the book, it wasn't as exciting, then you get to this part, and BANG!	Reads text to support own reaction. (Oral reading for a purpose.) Tabitha wants to share the reason for her sudden involvement with the novel.
Brenton You know when it said 'a horror grew over him'. I thought that meant the awful thing on the back of the book. I thought it was going to be that, but I kept on reading and it wasn't.	Brenton used cover illustration to help him make predictions, but self-corrected as text revealed further meaning.

Excerpts from Conference 2	Comments
Christine In the next chapter, I reckon the shadow will come back too. He'll have lots of scary adventures.	Christine immediately predicts what she thinks will happen.
Sasha I reckon Ged's going to become a really good wizard.	Sasha follows.
Dean W I think he's going to be a good wizard too — Ged that is — and he'll help everyone in Earthsea.	
David I think Ged is going to have a hard time with Jasper and he might have to have a contest or something.	All children are prepared to make predictions, thereby setting their own purposes for continued reading.
Christine Can we mark in where he went on the big map?	
Dean W I'll do it. He's travelled a long way now. He's gone from Gont — from the mountains in the middle of Gont — to that mage in Re-Albi.	As a result of Christine's request, the others were drawn into a discussion about Ged's physical journey and mapping. This confirmed that they were understanding the sequence of events.
Dean R They passed between some islands and, oh yeah, they went past Roke and then back up to it. They nearly missed it you know.	

Excerpts from Conference 4	**Comments**
(This conference was held after the children had finished reading chapter 6, 'Hunted' and chapter 7, 'The Hawk's Flight'.)	
David Ged got his second chance to name the Shadow Beast because Serret took him down into the dungeon and she said the stone would tell him anything — even the Shadow's real name.	After an opening question from the teacher, David recalled details and got the conference started.
Tabitha That's important, because he has to know the Shadow's real name if he wants to control it.	Comprehension of a key idea.
Dean R When I started reading about Serret, I got suspicious of her. As I kept reading, I knew she was bad news. I'm glad she got eaten by the birds. She was just trying to trick Ged. She tried to get Ged into trouble earlier on too, but I didn't realize that at the time.	Dean is showing what he understands about Serret's character.
Brenton Ogion said to Ged that he must 'turn around and hunt the hunter'.	
David Yeah — Ogion said that he didn't know where Ged should go, but he knew what Ged should do.	Brenton quotes text to make a point, and then David expands upon it.
Brenton He's got to turn around and face the Shadow if he's to have a chance.	
Tabitha But he's afraid, because he's already faced the Shadow twice and twice it's beaten him.	Tabitha explains Ged's fear.
Christine It's here on page 144. *(She reads out relevant parts.)*	Christine reads from text to support Tabitha's point.
Tabitha Third time he'll be lucky.	

Excerpts from Conference 4	**Comments**
Teacher What have we learned about Ged so far?	A 'following' question.
Christine He's brave, I think. But in the tower, he said he felt ashamed because he had kept running from the Shadow.	Both Christine and Dean offer answers. There are no 'right' or 'wrong' answers; both together add to the understanding of all the children in the group.
Dean R But he shouldn't be ashamed and he shouldn't be afraid — that's sensible.	
David In chapter 7, Ged said to Ogion that he had come back as he left. He called himself a fool. He was telling Ogion that he hadn't learned much at all and he was embarrassed. I felt sorry for him, but Ogion just smiled.	David also answers, but by referring to a specific chapter. He adds something about his own feelings and is very perceptive in picking up Ogion's response to Ged.
Dean W But in chapter 8 he finally goes hunting the Shadow.	Dean leads the discussion to chapter 8.
Tabitha He isn't as scared as he was before.	Tabitha recalls Ged's feelings and David gives his explanation. ('High level' comprehension; goes beyond actual text but quotes text for support.)
David That's because he made a decision. He said to Ogion, 'Master, I go hunting'.	
Sasha He reckons the best thing to do is fight him over the sea.	Recalling detail.
Teacher How would you compare Ged and the Shadow?	Teacher leads discussion towards the theme of the book.
Dean R Ged is good and the Shadow is bad. The Shadow stands for evil.	Dean explains theme in terms of 'good' and 'evil'.
Teacher What do you mean by 'stands for evil'?	

Excerpts from Conference 4	Comments

Dean R
Well . . . well, today it means people who murder and steal . . . bad people . . . the Shadow makes people bad.

Brenton
Today the Shadow is drugs and war and nuclear bombs.

Sasha
People have to do what Ged did. They have to turn and face these things. They are the people who are fighting all the bad things . . . good people like the police and the army and protesters.

Dean, Brenton and Sasha are relating the theme of "good and evil" to experiences of their own lives.

Christine
Can I read on page 165? After Ged's fight with the Shadow, it says: 'All terror was gone. All joy was gone. It was a chase no longer. He was neither hunted nor hunter, now.' Ged knew that there was no escape . . . he knew that they would meet again and he would wait.'

Oral reading for a purpose. A realization that the chase is over, but the battle is still to be won.

Dean R
It's hard to explain, but it was like good touching evil. And the good and the evil are equal in strength.

Dean struggling to articulate his own understanding of a key event.

Brenton
When evil chases good, it doesn't know the good's power, and then when it finds out, the evil backs off.

Brenton helping Dean and trying to clarify that event.

Dean W
You know when Ged went to the Inlet and he saw the Shadow — I thought it was really good the way Le Guin described the Shadow: 'a twisted man, deformed' — it sounded like jelly all going up and down.

Dean commenting on author's description and use of words; sharing of personal image of the Shadow.

David
I liked that too, but sometimes the author gives too much detail. I skimmed parts of the chapter, but really read the parts about the Shadow. Then, sometimes, I read quickly again.

David, like all competent and confident readers, sets his own purposes for reading and adjusts strategies and rate of reading to suit his purpose. David is also prepared to re-read when necessary. He 'explores' the text.

Excerpts from Conference 4	Comments
Brenton Yeah, there's a lot of detail. But the author knows heaps about islands and geography.	Brenton shows his understanding of what the author has to know to write the book.
Teacher How did you imagine the Shadow at first, and what do you think of it now?	Teacher's challenge.
Brenton When Ged first let out the Shadow, I imagined it like a Shadow on a wall. But now I feel it's like a blob of chewing gum that can stretch and grow.	Response. (Image changed.)
Teacher Me too.	Affirmation
Tabitha In one part, it said that, as the Shadow was coming towards Ged, the wind was blowing through it. It reminds me a bit about the Exorcist, because a girl had this evil thing in her body. It was doing what the Shadow is trying to do.	Tabitha's image develops further ideas about the Shadow.

Excerpts from Final Conference	Comments
Teacher What comments would you like to make about the overall theme of the book? *David* I'll just read this, because it says — 'Ged, by saying his own name, made the Shadow join him so he was whole again.' *(Read from own notes.)*You see, Ged said the Shadow's name, and the Shadow went into him. Vetch saw Ged's light grow dim, but it was still more powerful than the darkness. I thought that was the most important part.	David made notes before the conference started and was keen to share what he saw as the most important part: Ged overcoming the Shadow.
Brenton Well, I reckon it's one of the best books I've ever read, but I didn't think it would be for the first couple of chapters, because it took a while to get used to a lot of the words the author used for names. But it's a book about good and evil.	Brenton gives his judgement about the book ('one of the best', despite early difficulty). He states the theme simply and clearly.

Excerpts from Final Conference	Comments
Christine It says here *(and she referred to page 199)* 'I am whole, I am free'. Now Ged knew he was free.	Christine quotes text to refer to the resolution; perhaps also to refer to her own relief!
Dean W I thought it was good. They sailed back to Iffish and they were greated warmly by Yarrow. That makes the ending better, because it had been sad through the story and it makes it happier at the end.	Dean's expectation, that the ending would make sense and that the conflict would be resolved, is met.
Teacher I felt like that too. At last Ged had peace.	
Sasha At least we know that he doesn't have to fear the Shadow any more, because it's been destroyed.	
Teacher What are some of the minor themes running through the book?	
Christine It's about a boy who learns to be a Wizard, but his pride causes a Shadow Beast to follow him.	Christine, Sasha and Dean talk about minor themes of pride, friendship and making amends for mistakes.
Sasha Yes, he's scared, but he learns to face the Shadow or the evil. Vetch, his friend, helps him.	
Dean R It's about a boy who made a mistake that he wanted to undo.	
Teacher What have we learned about good and evil?	
David Not to always run from evil.	
Brenton Yeah, you have to learn to face bad things like Ged did.	
Sasha I learned that good always wins in the end.	

Excerpts from Final Conference	**Comments**
Dean R I learned that you might have courage, but you've got to be sensible as well, because courage may lead you to death. *Teacher* What did we learn about friendship? *Sasha* Vetch was a really good friend, because he went with Ged to find the Shadow even though Ged didn't want him to. *David* On page 175, it says *(reading text):* 'Pride was ever your mind's master'. Vetch was smiling, but he meant that Ged was too stubborn sometimes. *Tabitha* Sometimes Ged was too proud. He was too proud to accept things from other people, like . . . he said No at first about Vetch going with him. *Brenton* But Vetch thought he should go with Ged because others should know what happens. And also, he said that he was with Ged at the beginning and so he should be with him at the end. *Dean W* I really liked that. *Brenton* Ogion was also a great friend to Ged because he was always helping him and giving him advice. *Tabitha* He took Ged back and then helped him to make up his mind about turning around and hunting the Shadow.	Discussion of what children have learned; new insights; judgements based on children's own moral codes and value systems.

Excerpts from Final Conference	**Comments**
Sasha I think he was like a Father to Ged.	Appreciative identification with characters.
Christine He didn't get angry or anything with Ged, even when Ged said he had come back without learning anything.	
Dean R Ogion had been in the world a longer time than Ged, so he was more wise. He told Ged what *not* to do, as well as what to do.	
Teacher How did you feel while you were reading the book?	
Sasha For a couple of chapters, I kept thinking I was Ged and I was sitting in my room and I was doing in my head what he was doing while I was reading the books.	
Brenton I felt like that.	
David I felt like it when I read the Narnia series.	
Brenton When I was reading in my bed and I sank back, I kept on thinking I was floating on the sea.	
Dean R I felt like I was guiding Ged sometimes. Sometimes I'd read a bit and then think what might happen in the next few pages. When something like that did happen, I would think that I was guiding Ged.	Emotional responses to content and reactions to author's style involve all levels of comprehension: literal, inferential and evaluative. Responses here indicate a great deal of involvement with the story. Such involvement requires a high level of comprehension.
Dean W I want to read *The Tombs of Atuan* (one of the sequels to *A Wizard of Earthsea*).	
Christine I felt sad sometimes, and scared a bit. But then I was happy that he finally made it.	

References

Bloom, B. ed., *Taxonomy of Educational Objectives*, Longman Green, 1956.

Dalton, J., *Adventures in Thinking*, Nelson, 1985.

Graves, D., *Writing: Teachers and Children at Work*, Heinemann, 1984.

Holdaway, D., *Independence in Reading*, 2nd edn., Ashton Scholastic, 1980.

Huck, C., *Children's Literature in the Elementary School*, 3rd edn. updated, Holt, Rinehart and Winston, 1979.

Meek, M., *Learning to Read*, The Bodley Head, 1982.

Parry, J. & Hornsby, D., *Write On: A Conference Approach to Writing*, Martin Educational, 1985.

8 RESPONDING TO READING 3: ACTIVITIES AND SHARING

Putting Activities into Perspective

Children respond to what they have read in many different ways. Often, they will want to share their thoughts and feelings about a book they have just read. They may immediately prepare a poster advertising it to others, or they may choose one of many other activities possible. However, a child's response to a book may be to go to the library and find another book by the same author and to start reading it straight away. If further reading is the response, then the teacher should be thrilled, and there should never be any compulsion to complete an activity for the sake of completing an activity. **Reading itself always takes priority over activities.**

Activities must always be purposeful, and the child should know the purpose of the activity too. Activities can run the danger of becoming 'busy fill-ins' that neither result naturally from reading nor extend the reader's insight or enjoyment.

Some points to consider:
- Enjoyment is a top priority.
- Activities provide diverse forms of responding to reading; they may extend literature through art/craft, music, movement, drama, cooking, writing, games, and so on.
- Different forms of response suit different children and provide all with ways of expressing themselves.
- Children should be encouraged and helped to respond in different ways.
- The 'end result' of the activity is no more important than the participation and involvement of the children during the activity.

Why have Activities?

- The activity itself can be enjoyable.
- Reading itself is a solitary activity. Follow-up activities allow interaction between children (whether or not the same titles have been read).
- An activity can provide a 'breathing space' between books. (Have you never read a book that was so good that you just couldn't read another one until you had had a few days to savour it?)
- Activities can help the reader reflect upon the book read.
- Activities help other children to ask relevant questions of the reader.
- Activities give confidence to reluctant readers and reluctant sharers to take part.
- Activities form the basis for further questioning and discussion. The activities are often non-verbal but lead to further verbal responses which often extend well beyond earlier verbal responses.
- While the activities are being completed, the children are in one sense 'rehearsing' for later sharing.

Choosing Activities

The children are free to choose an activity, but the teacher has an important role to play in providing alternatives and guidelines. If there are no alternatives, there is no choice! If there are no guidelines, children may not link the purpose of the activity to the material read. It can be helpful to consider different activities with the whole class.

Early in the year, the teacher may wish to limit the number of activities from which the children choose. Then, a different activity could be added to the alternatives each week or so. Don't forget, one of the alternatives is to read another book! It can be useful to keep a growing class list of different activities. The children can refer to this for guidance. To assist the range of activities undertaken, a grid with activities on one axis and children's names on the other axis can be used. When the children complete a particular activity, they check off the grid shown on the following page.

Sometimes, teachers may specify the kind of activity which should be done. Such direction would be required when the teacher needs to challenge a particular child or group. It may also be required when the teacher wants the children to make links across curriculum areas or connections with previous reading activities or other aspects of the current reading program.

Activities to Extend Comprehension

The following levels of comprehension are taken from Barrett's Taxonomy and are used in this text as they are common categories and are useful in helping teachers to see a broad overview of directions in which children should be taken.

1 Literal
2 Re-organization and translation
3 Inferential
4 Evaluation
5 Appreciation

It is relatively easy to describe activities for the first two levels, but not as easy to describe activities for level 3 (inferential comprehension). It is increasingly difficult to have activities that develop comprehension at levels 4 and 5 since comprehension at levels 4 and 5 require much verbal interaction which is better harnessed during the conference and during share time.

The important consideration is that, as a result of the *involvement* in activities at levels 1, 2 and 3, readers will be given something concrete to help them extend their discussion and thereby their comprehension. (See Appendix 2 for an adaptation of Barrett's Taxonomy.)

ACTIVITIES	Drama	Models	Painting	Mobile	Book Reports	New Book Jacket	Poster	Radio Plays	Extension Research	Mural	Making a Game	Read Favourite Chapter to Class	Make a Comic Strip	Sculpture	Dress up as a Character	Making Masks	Make up a Song to Sing	Make a Kite Character	Character Cut Out	Write Brief Description of Character	Activity Sheet for Whole Grade	Poem	Wonder Word or Crossword	Pop-up	Tape Favourite Part
Paul		X																		X					
Dean.W.		X					X			X															
Marnie			X																						
Kristi		X					X									X									
Justin							X					X													
Brenton		X																					X		
Jackie		X					X																	X	
Deanne			X										X												
Amber			X				X						X												
Dean.R.		X																		X					
Glenn					X					X															
Ashley	X						X			X															
George		X																		X					
David					X	X																			
Leanne			X			X																			
Maree					X										X										
Tabitha			X				X																		
Tanya			X				X																		
Sasha		X											X											X	X
Christine			X															X							
Brendan					X									X											
Kylie		X					X																		
Kaine							X																		
Michelle B	X	X														X									
Trudi																									
Rebecca			X				X																		
Matthew		X																							
Brett							X																		
Deborah									X															X	
Michelle F			X	X																					X

Purpose of Activity: Literal Comprehension

1.1 Recognition of detail
- mobile of main characters
- mural depicting details of setting(s)

1.2 Recognition of main idea
- individual children jot down what they consider to be 3 important points and then compare their points with another child; partners negotiate to reduce their combined 6 points down to what they consider to be the 3 most important points.

1.3 Recognition of a sequence
- draw a cartoon strip with frames showing the main events in sequence (restrict the number of frames to suit the book).

1.4 Recognition of comparisons
- tabulate obvious comparisons (e.g. good/bad, important/unimportant, strong/weak); compare characters, events, settings, moods.
- tabulate obvious comparisons across titles (or authors); when comparisons are made across books, they can include comparisons of style, plot and illustrations.

1.5 Recognition of cause and effect
- match illustrations of cause with written cards describing the effect (or vice versa).

1.6 Recognition of character traits
- children choose extracts from music which portrays a particular character's personality.
- select percussion instruments and compose three or four bars of music to portray a character's mood.

Purpose of Activity: Translation and/or Reorganization of Ideas and Information

2.1 Classifying
- compile lists or charts to show
  People Places Things
- add your title, author or illustrator to displayed lists in the classroom e.g. humorous authors; poets; picture story books; science fiction.

2.2 Outlining
- use semantic webbing to give an outline of story structure or character links (see chapter 11).
- write statements on cards and use these for sorting games.

2.3 Summarizing
- retell the story, in your own words, and record on audio tape.
- make a matchbox book (this requires a heavily summarized story and miniature illustrations).

2.4 Synthesizing
- create an acrostic by using the letters of a character's name to start words which describe the character; where possible, use words from the text.

Purpose of Activity: Inferential Comprehension

While there are activities which support the inferences readers make, inferential comprehension is more easily covered through questioning and discussion. Therefore, the conference situation is better for developing this form of comprehension than independent activities.

3.1 Inferring supporting detail
   • defend your belief about a character by finding relevant sections of text (to be read aloud) which will support your view.

3.2 Inferring main idea
   • partners play the 'Say Something' game. Each child silently reads a paragraph or page. Each in turn then has to say something brief about the author's main message. They read on and continue in this way. (Readers get immediate feedback about their inferences.)
   • list briefly the things you think the author had to know to write this book.

3.3 Inferring sequence
   • write a different ending for your book.
   • take an incident that ocurs in the book and act out a different reaction to the incident which could still occur in the flow of events (for example, what else could Sophie have said or done after the B.F.G. actually snatched her from her bed).

3.4 Inferring comparisons
   • draw 'split-screen' images of a character or a setting as they appear 'then and now' or 'here and there'. (For example, Abigail from *Playing Beatie Bow* in her 19th century setting and her 20th century setting.)
   • by means of 'thought bubbles', show what two different characters are thinking about a particular situation or incident.

3.5 Inferring cause and effect relationships, character traits, motivation and interaction
   • a small group of children who have read a common title pantomime an event from the story and others in the class have to infer what has happened, why it happened, what could happen next.

3.6 Predicting outcomes
   • strips of card, separated into, say, five frames are supplied. The first three frames contain statements about events from a story; children supply the last two frames.
   (Alternatively, this activity may be done with a combination of print and pictures.)

3.7 Interpreting figurative language
   • children find figures of speech in their book and interpret them literally through illustrations (for example, 'It rained cats and dogs').

The artwork is used as a basis for discussion about similies and metaphors and how they might have evolved.

Purpose of Activity: Evaluation and Appreciation

The 'activities' for the following levels of comprehension are actually the conference itself and the share time, as these levels of comprehension require much verbal interaction. These levels of comprehension cannot be attained by non-verbal activities on their own, as opinions, values, past experiences and moral codes are involved. (Non-verbal activities do not get at these things, but they may help individual readers *towards* these things.)

Evaluation

4.1 Judgements of reality and fantasy

Could the story have happened? What other books have you read like this one?

4.2 Judgements of fact or opinion

What is the author trying to make you think? Can you identify the author's purpose for writing?

4.3 Judgements of appropriateness

Does the author give enough information about . . .? What part of the story best describes the main character/setting?

4.4 Judgements of worth, desirability and acceptability

Was the character right or wrong in what he/she did? Was the character's behaviour good or bad?

Appreciation

5.1 Emotional response to content

How did you feel? What was your favourite part?

5.2 Identification with characters and incidents
   - empathy
   - sensitivity
   - sympathy

Why did you feel that way? Did that part/character remind you of anything that has happened to you?

5.3 Reactions to author's use of language
   - style
   - imagery

What words did the author use to make you feel the way you did? What memorable pictures has the author made in your mind?

Activities Related to Elements of a Story

Taken from: *Now Read On*, revised edn. 1985, Dept. of English Language and Literature, Victoria College, Burwood.

Exploring Character

Teaching Points

- What characters are like.
- How a writer presents characters.
- How and why characters develop.
- How we feel about characters.
- How characters reflect moral qualities and values.

Activities

- Making a progressive list of words/phrases to describe character.
- Writing description of, or opinion of, or feelings about a character at beginning of book. Then writing the same when book is finished. Compare the two. Has the character changed? Have your feelings about the character changed? Why?
- Making a time-line of a character's life or development as story progresses.
- Presenting character visually and/or in writing in the form of
  free verse,
  a 'wanted' poster,
  an epitaph,
  a portrait (perhaps for inclusion in a photograph album),
  a puppet,
  a description through the eyes of another character.
- Writing a question to ask a character and posting it in a question box during serial reading. Use questions for discussion at end of book.
- Television Show — 'This is Your Life'.
- Trial of character.
- Interview; press conference.
- Diary writing.
- Raft Debate.
- Writing letters between
  two characters,
  the reader and a character,
  a character and the author.

Exploring Setting

Teaching Points
- How a writer creates vivid word pictures (e.g. use of senses, imagery, colour, detail, contrast, point of view).
- How atmosphere and mood are created and used.
- How the setting of a story is important, and how it is linked with character and plot.
- How to transfer verbal description into visual presentation and to transfer a visual image effectively into words.

Activities
- Presenting setting visually as
  a map showing a journey,
  a grid map or picture built up progressively as story is read,
  a travel brochure or poster,
  a class mural, collage or montage,
  a backdrop for a puppet play,
  embroidery, weaving,
  3D model.
- Collecting and discussing imagery used by writer. Making up own imagery to use in descriptive writing.
- Describing a setting from different viewpoints.
- Discussing descriptive passages to see how a writer has made them vivid. Then using the same devices in writing.
- Making progressive charts of descriptive words, to use later as a basis for writing.
- Drawing word pictures in form of
  free verse,
  'for sale' ad or poster,
  travel brochure.

Exploring Plot

Teaching Points
- How a story is structured.
- Predicting possible outcomes.
- How the author uses conflict to create suspense, and how conflict is resolved.

Activities

- Summarizing the story progressively in the form of
  a time-line in words and/or pictures,
  chapter names,
  a story ladder,
  a list of key words.
- Making a pictorial record of all or part of the story in the form of
  a mural,
  a map or illustration,
  a 3D presentation.
- Dramatizing an event in the book as
  a play,
  a puppet play,
  a tape-recorded dialogue.
- Writing another episode for a book that is episodic.
- Writing a prologue or epilogue.
- Writing about an event in a different way as
  a letter,
  a newspaper report,
  a diary,
  a ship's log,
  a first person narration by two different characters.
- Making a book jacket or a poster advertising the book.

Exploring Theme

Themes are the central ideas of a book, the statements it makes about life. They are expressed through the lives of the characters, through the things that they do in the settings in which they are placed. Obviously, then, many of the preceding activities on character, setting and plot will help to explore themes.

Themes in books for children deal with aspects of life that are relevant to children. They deal with the need to belong; with friendship and loneliness; with learning to cope in a world that is exciting and strange; with growing up and finding one's place in the world; with the acceptance of death and of the fact that life goes on. Children have a strong sense of justice, and books in which good overcomes evil, and virtue and heroism are rewarded form a large part of the literature for children.

Exploring Style

Readers develop an awareness of a writer's style as they consider the 'how' of the story, as they explore the ways in which he has used language to create his story.

Again, some of the preceding activities, particularly those that involve careful consideration of the text, will contribute to this awareness, as will points raised in discussion.

References

Teachers and children are familiar with many activities, but there are several excellent references to consult when you want to introduce something new. Several of these are listed in the References at the end of this chapter.

Required Comments and the Reading Log

Why should the teacher require the children to write comments? Some considerations are:

- It can prepare them for individual and group conferences.
- It helps them to put thoughts and feelings into written form.
- It helps them to become aware of different responses.
- It builds up to provide a very useful 'Reading Log'.
- It can promote thought about issues not previously considered (writing is 'hands-on' thinking).

Children may be required to write *brief* comments after any reading material they have read or have attempted to read.

> Teachers must use their knowledge of individual children and their common sense to determine when they will require brief written comments of them.

It is important to emphasize that the comments are *brief.* The requirements may be: title of the book (or selection) as a heading; information about the author and/or illustrator; own comment. This is a requirement even if the children decide not to finish reading the material. If this is the case, their comments must explain why they decided not to continue reading.

Providing Guidelines and Assistance

For inexperienced readers who have not had opportunities to develop their responses to reading, the 'Required Comments' can be difficult. Teachers need to provide guidelines and assistance. If necessary, this can be provided daily as the Introductory Activity with the whole class, until the children have an understanding of what is required. For specific children having difficulty with the commentary, teaching groups can be organized for this purpose.

Sheets with guiding questions can be provided. Samples of these sheets are supplied as reproducible pages in Appendix 1. Note that these are **Guiding Questions only.** Children do *not* have to answer the questions. They may choose to answer one or two or just to read through the questions for ideas. Once children know what is required, or feel confident of making their own comments, they can do without the sheets altogether or just refer to them when they need to.

The form and length of the child's response will vary according to the material read, the child's comprehension, the child's purpose for reading in the first place, the teacher's intention and the purpose for keeping the record. The required comments may be written before attending a conference or starting an activity. However, if children are having difficulty, they could attend a conference first. During the conference, the teacher can help the children determine what they wish to comment on.

Examples of Required Comments

The following accounts indicate how variable the written comments might be and give some hints about how the children might have used the question sheets ('Thinking About My Reading').

Julia:

10-year-old Julia read *Tales of a Fourth Grade Nothing* by Judy Blume and because of the relationship between Peter and his younger brother Fudge, she decided that the emphasis of her written comments would be on characterization. Also, brief attention was given to the author's intentions.

George:

9-year-old George read *The Magic Finger* by Roald Dahl and decided to consider the 'plot questions'. He also answered the question 'What is the author trying to tell us?' as there was such a strong message about how we treat animals. Because he enjoyed *The Magic Finger*, he went on to read another Dahl book, *The BFG*. He commented on setting, using questions from that section as a guide. He then answered the question, 'Were there any unusual ways of saying things?' because the BFG (Big Friendly Giant) had peculiar language.

Effie:

8-year-old Effie read the picture-story book, *The Lighthouse Keeper's Lunch*, by Rhonda and David Armitage. She wrote a comment on the record sheet in her reading folder *(The way in which the lighthouse keeper's wife sent him his lunch reminded me of the flying fox at Camp Adanac and I liked the way the author used bubbles for the birds talking.)* The teacher did **not** require her to follow the question sheet.

Matthew:

11-year-old Matthew read a magazine article about the training of police in the motorcycle school. His comments related to the question about what he had learned from reading the article and to a question about what he still wanted to know.

Often, the comments are written in an ordinary exercise book. If they are written on index cards, they can be filed as a class collection. This collection provides a 'data base' to which other readers in the room can refer. The reverse side of the card can be used for other readers to make comments or to record points of agreement or disagreement.

These cards can also be used to group children for conferences and as an information source during the conference. If a computer is available, then the compilation of a data base will be more efficient and its use more flexible.

HERMAN THE GREAT

By Zora Olsen.

This book was Unreal.

It was Unreal because Herman went on a lot of exciting adventures. I thought the best adventure was when Herman flew across the U.S.A. Herman couldn't see in the fog and crashed at the bottom of the Grand Canyon.

When Herman was flying the plane I thought of My Uncle Steve because he makes model planes and flys them.

I felt like I wanted to do what Herman did.

Matthew. Year 4

The Folk Of The

Faraway Tree.   ENID BLYTON

What Paul Thinks Of It..............
I thought the Book was very
exciting. There were lots of
adventures. They were great to.
The book has most of my best
book Charictors.
I liked all of the book really.
I could amagine the pictures
in my head. Now I would like
to redd....... The Curse Of
The Egyptian Mummy.   Year 2

Space Shuttles.

This book is about space shuttles. It did not tell me how space shuttles take off.

Nathan   Year 2

Roxann

The Patchwork Cat.

Nicola Bayley + William Mayne .

The cat is the main characteR. He lost his home and the milk man found him and took him home.

Sharing

Share Time is for Publication!

Publication in reading? Yes. To share is to make something public. When children share their responses to reading with an 'audience', they are making those responses public.

Just as writers may get to the stage of publishing their piece of writing in some form or another, readers also 'publish' their responses to reading.

Share Time is a necessary conclusion to every reading session. Early in the year, the teacher will need to provide assistance to get this part of the session going. Teachers can make suggestions to individual children about the different ways in which they might prepare for sharing what they have been reading. During Share Time itself, the teacher will also need to help by asking questions of the child sharing. This will provide a model for the other children (as it does during the Introductory Activity) so that they learn about the different kinds of comments and questions that will make Share Time valuable.

What are the Values of Share Time?

1   Values for child or group sharing:
  a   developing habits of reacting to reading
  b   seeing the necessity of planning for share time
  c   developing audience reading skills
  d   selecting appropriate parts for sharing
  e   enjoying the attention of peers as they participate in the sharing and encourage the reader; 'feeling good'
  f   learning to take criticisms and use them positively
  g   developing ability to answer questions
  h   gaining greater awareness of audience expectations
  i   developing confidence.

2   Values to audience
  a   developing ability to listen
  b   becoming more aware of others' appreciation of literature
  c   learning to accept or reject recommendations made by others
  d   becoming aware of reading materials they don't choose to read themselves
  e   recognizing that others can enjoy something you don't enjoy yourself
  f   evaluating peers' judgements, opinions, values
  g   learning the difference between constructive and destructive criticism
  h   learning what kinds of comments and questions produce the most information for the audience
  i   incidental learning about characterization, theme, plot, style, and so on
  j   building of a co-operative community spirit.

As Share Time develops through the year, the teacher's role changes. Initially, teachers need to organize and guide the children. However, as soon as possible, the children must take the initiative and responsibility for the session.

Jackie — Year 5, Mill Park Primary School
Jackie read *The Birthday* by Mary Cockett and in Share Time, she presented her papier mâché model of a birthday cake, answered questions that were asked and then promised to make a real cake for the class.

When a chocolate cake finally arrived at school, the children asked the teacher to read them "Chocolate Cake" by Michael Rosen, which was a favourite poem of theirs. So, as they ate, they heard the poem about a little boy who creeps downstairs, steals into the fridge and starts systematically eating a whole chocolate cake. Of course, he thinks he's just evening up the edges! The children, with mouths full of chocolate cake, listened to the poem that could really have been written about them!

George — Year 5, Mill Park Primary School.
George had been a slow, reluctant reader, but responded amazingly to a literature-based, conference approach to reading.

During 'Share Time' at the end of a reading session in Term 3, all children were seated to listen to George present *Herman the Great* by Zora Olsen.

George had read the book after Matthew had recommended it to him and the two of them stood before the class proudly exhibiting a model of the aeroplane that Herman (the main character) had flown.

George confidently talked about the theme of the book and why he liked Herman so much. Various children questioned him and it was heartening to see how he responded, as he had been a very reluctant reader who also lacked confidence.

When one child asked George about the part he liked best, George surprised everyone in the room by declaring that he would read the best part out. He quickly found the section he wanted, explained to everyone the overall story and how this part fitted into it, and then read clearly and confidently. That alone was a 'first' for George, and he was clearly pleased with himself. However, the best was yet to come.

When George finished, all the children spontaneously applauded him. Then they all wanted to talk at once. 'George, that's fantastic!' 'Hasn't he improved, Mrs Sukarna?' George's response was, 'You'll have to wait until I've finished the *Machine Gunners* and I'll read some of that too!'

It was a very special moment for everyone, but especially for George. He felt good about himself and all the children shared his feelings. This experience of success was one of similar experiences which convinced George that he *could read*, that he *did* enjoy it and that led him to become an enthusiastic reader.

References

Bailes, J. (ed), *The Reading Bug and How to Catch It*, Ashton Scholastic, 1980.

Barrett, T., 'Taxonomy of Cognitive and Affective Dimensions of Reading Comprehension', unpublished paper, 1968.

Canterford, B., *Storyline*, Shepparton Teachers' Centre, 1980.

Canterford, B., *More Storyline*, Shepparton Teachers' Centre, 1984.

Education Department of Victoria publication, *Happily Ever After*, 1975.

Gilmour, H., & Tyrer, D, *Reading On*, Education Department of Victoria, 1985.

Huck, C., *Children's Literature in the Elementary School*, 3rd edn. updated, 1979, Holt, Rinehart and Winston, 1979.

Johnson, T., & Louis, D., *Literacy Through Literature*, Methuen, 1985.

Polette, N., & Hamlin, M., *Exploring Books with Gifted Children*, Libraries Unlimited, Inc., 1980.

Sutherland, Z., & Arbuthnot, M., *Children and Books*, 5th edn, Scott Foresman, 1977.

9 READING SKILLS AND STRATEGIES

Introduction

First and foremost, children must discover and enjoy books. They must be given time to select and quietly read all kinds of material. It is only when they enjoy books that children gain momentum and have a drive to develop skills.

Skills in Context

The learning of skills is much more efficient when the learner sees the need to attend to them. Given a rich and varied reading program, children do discover for themselves the skills they need to master. (Of course, the teacher is the major influence on the type of reading program being offered and is thus responsible for putting the children in situations where they *are* confronted with the need to attend to skills.)

Also, the 'teaching time' required to help children with skills is greatly reduced when the children themselves see the importance of mastering such skills.

When appropriate, reading skills and strategies will be specifically attended to and developed
- during shared readings;
- during the reading conference (which is very much a comprehension session); and
- in teaching groups.

The major purpose of instruction is to make the children more *aware* of the information on the page and the strategies for handling that information.

Readers employ various strategies to interpret information available in reading materials. The following diagram helps us to understand what is involved, but other references which should be consulted include:

- Goodman, Y. & Burke, C., *Reading Strategies: Focus on Comprehension*, Holt, Rinehart & Winston, 1980.

- Johnson, T. & Louis, D., *Literacy Through Literature*, Nelson, 1985.

- Latham, R. & Sloan, P., *A Modern View of Reading*, Nelson, 1979.

- Smith, F., *Reading*, Cambridge University Press, 2nd edn., 1986.

- Articles from the *Language Arts* journal (National Council of Teachers of English); *The Reading Teacher* (International Reading Association) and the *Australian Journal of Reading* (Australian Reading Association).

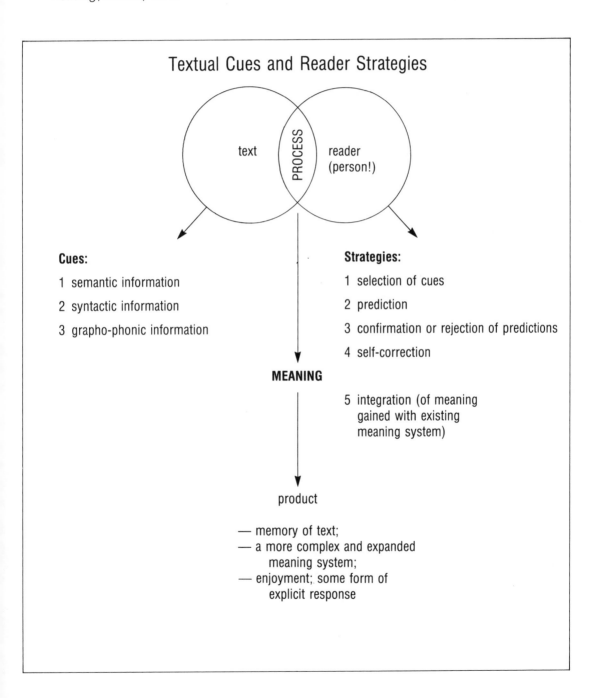

Textual Cues and Reader Strategies

text   PROCESS   reader (person!)

Cues:

1 semantic information

2 syntactic information

3 grapho-phonic information

Strategies:

1 selection of cues

2 prediction

3 confirmation or rejection of predictions

4 self-correction

MEANING

5 integration (of meaning gained with existing meaning system)

product

— memory of text;
— a more complex and expanded meaning system;
— enjoyment; some form of explicit response

Comprehension

Pearson and Johnson (1978) have written about the 'confused world of reading comprehension' and suggest five causes of this confusion:

1 **Poor terminology** We use different words to describe the same thing. We like to use our own jargon or terminology and this is a source of confusion.
2 **Redundancy** Lists of so-called comprehension skills give the impression that 'each skill has a separate and equal identity when, in fact, they are either highly interrelated or different names for the same thing.'
3 **Fuzzy distinctions** Some skills are classified as comprehension skills in one system and as word identification skills in another.
4 **Extremes of belief** These range from the assertion that comprehension cannot be taught to the belief that it can.
5 **Process and product issues** It is this last cause of confusion that we wish to take up in more detail here.

Comprehension as a Process and as a Product

'Comprehension as a *process* is an elusive entity. It is what happens to readers *as they read*. It is what keeps them going when they read . . . It is what has broken down when we say to ourselves, "It's all Greek to me." or "I can't take it any longer . . ." Comprehension as a *product* is not so elusive. On the other hand, we wonder about its importance.' (Pearson and Johnson, 1978, p.5.)

If we see comprehension as the end product of reading, then we ask children questions or administer one of many tests. However, what we are doing is testing their *memory* of what they comprehended. The actual comprehension occured *during* the reading. We would argue that the phrase 'comprehension as a product' can be misleading. Perhaps what writers mean by 'comprehension as a product' is 'memory of comprehension', or something similar.

Since the end *product* can be more or less measured, it has been the product that has been traditionally emphasized, despite differing opinions about its importance.

Even though the world of comprehension is a confused one, we certainly do not wish to take an extreme position. Already there are too many false dichotomies in educational argument. Certainly, both process and product are important:

Comprehension Which Occurs *During* Reading
is Important
and
'Memory of Comprehension' *After* Reading
is Important.

However, traditional practice has given most, if not all, attention to the latter. At least we can argue here that equal attention be given to both.

Important comprehension skills are involved when employing strategies such as prediction, confirmation, rejection and self-correction. Perhaps it would not be wrong to call these strategies comprehension skills. We can certainly help children predict, confirm or reject their predictions, and self-correct. By so doing, we are developing their ability to comprehend *while* they read. We can also continue to test their memory of comprehension in ways ranging from informal chats to formal tests (so long as the latter are **valid** and **reliable!**) It is our experience that teachers gain more information about a reader's comprehension during a conference than from any test. In addition it is extremely difficult to find a test that is both valid and reliable.

Implications for Teaching

What, then, is the teacher's role? How can teachers provide the necessary balance between *developing* comprehension and *testing memory* of comprehension?

Traditionally, memory of comprehension has been tested by having children answer a series of comprehension questions (from the chalkboard, from S.R.A. cards, from kits, from purple sheets, and so on). This is still sometimes appropriate, but must be done in the name of testing *memory* of comprehension.

> To develop comprehension abilities, the teacher must intervene *during* the reading process.

It is a common but misguided belief that 'progressive' teachers do not teach; that they are simply available, like smiling supermarket managers, so that children may roam the educational environment and pick from the shelves what they wish. This is not so. **The teacher's role must be to intervene.** Intervention will occur at any appropriate time, but particularly during introductory activities, conference sessions and teaching groups. Intervention will thus be both spontaneous *and* planned.

In fact, intervention *during* the learning processes is one of the factors which distinguishes 'progressive' teachers from 'entrenched' teachers. It is the attention to *both* process and product which distinguishes the former from the latter. (Of course, good teachers have always attended to both.)

Word Recognition

There are several factors involved in word recognition:
- sight vocabulary
- context
- structural analysis
- phonics
- outside references.

Each of these provides a way to recognize words and will be discussed briefly in turn. For further discussion, readers are encouraged to turn to the references listed below:

Hittleman, D., *Developmental Reading: A Psycholinguistic Perspective*, Rand McNally College Publishing Company, 1978.

Holdaway, D., *Independence in Reading*, Ashton Scholastic, 2nd edn., 1980.

Johnson, D. & Pearson, P., *Teaching Reading Vocabulary*, Holt, Rinehart & Winston, 1978.

Johnson, T. & Louis, D., *Literacy through Literature*, Methuen, 1985.

Sloan, P. & Latham, R., *Teaching Reading Is . . . .* Nelson, 1981.

The term 'word recognition' and other terms such as word identification, word attack and decoding are all used loosely and often incorrectly. Hittleman (1978) clarifies the muddle for us: '*word recognition* indicates the processes by which a reader realizes what word an author has used and the meaning intended for it.' In other words, readers recognize a word when they understand what the *author* meant it to mean. The word, of course, will usually have other meanings (particularly if it is a 'content' word rather than a 'function' word).

Sight Vocabulary

Children must be given every opportunity to quickly build up a basic sight vocabulary. It stands to reason that the more words children can recognize in a text, the more context clues they will be able to draw upon for working out the unknown words.

This does *not* mean that a list of words should be taught in isolation. An initial sight vocabulary can be built up informally through:
- teacher-made books
- classroom charts
- signs and labels
- teacher's written records of words or phrases commonly used by the children in classroom talk
- language-experience activities
- caption books
- use of written forms of songs, poems, and nursery rhymes that are well known orally.

Holdaway (1980, Appendix B) has developed a procedure for helping early readers quickly develop a basic sight vocabulary. We have used this procedure with children in the first years at school with dramatic success. It is a 'game-like' procedure requiring some work to set up, but the effort is well worthwhile.

Context

Reading is a thinking process by which the reader makes meaning. When a word is not recognized, meaning-making may be slowed down.

One powerful way of maintaining meaning-making is to make predictions from context. To do this the reader can employ both visual and non-visual information. The visual information on the page includes the text itself, the words which are recognized and any supporting pictorial information. Younger readers in particular may rely heavily on the pictorial cues to remind them of developing meaning. At a very early stage of reading, there is a reliance on picture cues (such as the size of the Billy Goat Gruff) to trigger meanings in the developing story. This is understandable. The teacher must use the information that the readers get from the pictures to help them make more meaning from the text itself. (It is a basic educational premise that we work from the **known** to the **unknown.**) Mature readers may also need to use context cues such as illustrations, graphs, charts and maps. In *A Wizard of Earthsea* Ged's journey is much easier to understand when one refers to the maps. The maps provided in *The Hobbit* are also important aids to understanding. In informational books, illustrations are sometimes essential to grasp the meaning of particular terms used. Teaching groups should often be used to help children use these illustrations in conjunction with the text. Picture-story books (including those for older children) can **not** be read without giving proper attention to the pictures, because the text is not meant to stand on its own. The pictures embellish and extend the meaning of the text.

In addition to the visual information available to the readers, there is a vast store of non-visual information available if **meaningful material** is used. Meaningful material makes sense; it tells a 'story' or tells about something; it touches the readers in a personal way; it enables readers to identify with it in some way or to relate it to their own experience or knowledge or feelings. If the material allows readers to use what *they* know, then meaning is grasped much more easily.

Context cues are very powerful word recognition cues. It surprises many readers to learn that some of the most helpful information for recognizing a word comes not from the word itself, but from all the printed information around that word!

Context certainly determines the meaning a particular word has, but context does not always *reveal* what that meaning is. When context does not help readers recognize words, and when word recognition is slowing down the making of meaning, then other strategies must be used.

When context does help recognition of a word, only one of the word's meanings is revealed. The word may have other meanings not revealed in the present context. This should not be seen as a limitation, as the immediate need of a reader is only to determine the author's meaning within that context.

When sight vocabulary and use of context cues still do not allow sufficiently rapid making of meaning, then using cues from within the unkown word itself may help. Readers should search for known word parts (structural analysis) or known phonic elements. When this also fails, then readers should ask someone else. Sloan and Latham (1981) warn us that mechanical phonic analysis and consulting others require less thinking about meaning, and it becomes too easy to use these strategies despite their inefficiency. 'What is significant is the fact that these non-thinking strategies are observable and, in the minds of teachers, easily structured for teaching.' (p.55) As a result, children learn that word accuracy is more important than meaning.

Phonics

An alphabetic system uses letters as symbols for speech sounds, so it *is* possible for readers to use letter-sound relationships to help with the recognition of words. Unfortunately, the correspondences between letters and sounds are frail, so letter-sound relationships do not always help. However, if we help children to know that **letter-sound relationships lead to 'possibilities, not certainties',** then phonics instruction is both possible and important. (Durkin, 1974.)

Two main purposes for learning phonic generalizations are:

1. When readers develop a systematic way of attacking words they are unsure of, one of the things they should do is check their prediction against the first letter or letter cluster of the word. (See 'A Strategy for Word Attack' p.104) It is essential to learn phonic generalizations in order to be able to do this checking.

2. If readers are unable to predict what a written word is, they may be able to turn the unknown graphic form of the word into sound. If they are then able to pronounce it correctly, they may recognize the word aurally.

Principles in Teaching Phonics

1 The letter-sound relationships must be taught within the context of words and sentences. Sounds in isolation become very artificial and distorted.

2 Teaching should be planned so that children learn by induction. That is, after considering various examples, they develop (with help from the teacher) their own generalizations. Words are selected from shared-book experiences, language-experience stories, wall charts, children's stories, and so on, so that these specific words are used to help children arrive at a generalization about the way a sound common to all of them is recorded. (Children *know* the sounds; they have to learn which letters we use to represent those sounds.)

Early readers need an inductive approach because known words are used to teach the letter-sound relationships they have in common. Inductive teaching helps all children acquire an approach to learning which encourages them to look at words they know and determine for themselves phonic generalizations which have not been *taught*. However, teachers should also respond in ways which seem appropriate for any current situation, and it may occasionally be appropriate to teach deductively — to provide a generalization and have children find examples. However, as Durkin (1974) reminds us, this is a telling rather than a reasoning process.

3 Letter-sound relationships are taught as *one of several* word recognition strategies.

Structural Analysis

If we look at how words are structured, we sometimes get information which helps to gain meaning.

Structural analysis is a skill in which a word's meaningful parts are studied. Children are helped to look for familiar word parts within words that are unfamiliar.

Structural analysis includes a study of
• base words (or root words)
• prefixes and suffixes
• inflectional endings
• compound words
• contractions.

Base Words (root words)

Structural analysis is sometimes called morphemic analysis. Morphemes are the smallest units of meaning in language. For example, 'boy' is a single morpheme which can stand on its own and is therefore referred to as a free morpheme. 'Boys' contains the free morpheme 'boy' and the bound morpheme 's' (meaning plural).

Since morphemes, like words, derive their meaning from the context in which they are used, morphemic analysis or structural analysis must be combined with context analysis.

Like phonic analysis, it cannot be used in isolation. Unlike phonic analysis, structural analysis has a high degree of consistency. Consider the word 'touch'. The phonic elements 'ou' and 'ch' do *not* have consistent pronunciations;

>   ou — tough, out, route, although, roup
>   (rōōp), pour, tour, tousle
>   ch — chocolate, chrome, chalet

However, as a structural unit (base word), the word 'touch' has a single pronunciation (tŭch) and its meaning is predictable whether by itself or in words like touches, touching, untouchable, touched, and so on.

Prefixes and Suffixes

As children come across words in their reading materials that include prefixes or suffixes, these can be noted and added to class lists or charts. Word building games can be played by adding prefixes or suffixes to known base words. However, it is *not* helpful to teach lists and require memory of meanings. Again, the reading materials used will dictate which words and meaningful word parts (morphemes) are studied. It can never be the other way around.

A useful reference is *Springboards: Ideas for Spelling* (Snowball and Bolton, 1985).

Many prefixes, base words and suffixes come from ancient languages, such as Latin and Greek. Many books, such as *Teaching Reading Vocabulary* (Johnson and Pearson, 1978), have ideas for helping children learn these elements in interesting and entertaining ways.

Inflectional Endings

Inflectional endings are added to words to show grammatical changes. Children who have learned to speak a language use inflectional endings quite naturally. For example, children will add an 's' to a noun to make a plural (they will sometimes do this inappropriately, as in 'mouses' or 'sheeps'). They will add 'ing' to a verb to make a participle or to show tense (jump — jumping).

Inflectional endings are added to:	to show:
nouns	number, gender and case;
verbs	participles, tense, third-person singular, progressive form;
adverbs	degree
adjectives	comparison

Compound Words

Children also use compound words easily and naturally in their everyday language use. English has many compound words and recognition of them may be simplified for children if we show them the individual words that make up the compound word. Again, many 'general method' texts provide ideas and teaching activities.

Use of Outside References

'Outside' references include dictionaries, thesauri and any other resource books, but also any useful people — peers, parents, teachers!

Dictionaries and thesauri are often used as a 'last resort' for several reasons:

1 they require quite sophisticated skills to be used properly;
2 they interrupt the reading of the text and detract from ongoing meaning-making;
3 they give definitions or synonyms but may not give the author's intended meaning.

In the early stages of reading development, few dictionaries or thesauri are manageable. Even the simplest of them requires a certain reading ability. Nevertheless, teachers should help young children to learn the skills which will later help them to use such reference books.

The Major Purposes of Instruction

As stated in the opening of this chapter, a major purpose of instruction is to make the children more **aware** of:

- the information available to them on the page;
- the strategies for handling that information.

Balance in the Use of Cues and Strategies

Text contains three sources of information:

- semantic
- syntactic
- graphophonic

These sources of information or cueing systems are well documented and will not be described here.

It is the responsibility of teachers to ensure that children use all three of these cueing systems. When children depend on one, they must be shown how the others can help them. For example, if children over-rely on context (semantic, syntactic and pictorial cues) and guess wildly at words, then they must be helped to use graphophonic information to check their predictions. If they over-rely on graphophonic information and plod through text bit by bit, then they have to be helped to see how important context cues are and be given practice using them.

It is essential that children ask themselves at least two questions while reading:

1 Does it make   (refers to semantics)
   sense to me?
2 Does it sound   (refers to syntax)
   right?

If the answer to either question is 'No', then children need to know what to do. First, they should be given the opportunity to help themselves. They may need to re-read, see if pictorial cues help, check their word identification, possibly even use a dictionary.

Instruction should help children discover that prediction (informed guessing) is not only acceptable, but is encouraged. Often, older brothers and sisters, or sometimes parents and teachers, have told children not to guess! The spirit of 'have a go' is important in all learning, including reading. If children predict incorrectly, they must also know that they should not stop and give up. They must be encouraged to self-correct and must be given *time* to self-correct before someone jumps in quickly and takes the opportunity away from them.

Fostering Independence

When children are having difficulty with reading, a common practice of the teachers is to jump in, take more control and make more corrections for them. Consequently, slow readers come to expect that the 'helper' *will* jump in. One result of this is that text is fragmented, there is no 'flow' of language, and there is a loss of 'semantic coherence'. Such children also give up control and believe that they are unable to read without 'being plugged into another person' (Holdaway, 1980).

One of the sad consequences of this is that the slow readers have less opportunity to learn to read by reading. 'Too many humane and supportive remedial programmes emphasizing the hearing (and correcting) of oral reading perpetuate or magnify dependence.' (Holdaway, 1980. p.209.)

If children are to be independent, we must help them learn procedures or strategies that allow them to 'have a go' on their own. The 'Strategy for Word Attack' (see following page) is one which helps readers to be independent.

Mastery

Instruction must also ensure that children master skills so that their use becomes automatic. While skills are being learned, they must be reinforced time and time again. In the early years of school, this is best done through successive readings of the same material and by providing the children with activities which have been specially designed to practise certain skills. Many commercial materials are useful (see the final section of this chapter) but the activities will also need to be planned and prepared by the teacher.

In summary, instruction must ensure that:

- children become independent (that is, they are prepared to 'have a go')
- children use all three textual cues available
- children know what to do when they are unsure (unsure of meaning; unsure of a word)
- children get plenty of practice so that skills become automatic.

A Strategy for Word Attack

Often, when inexperienced readers come to a word they don't recognize, they have no strategy or plan for dealing with the word. They might stare at the word (or even the ceiling!). If they only know how to 'sound out' words, and the word is one of the many English words that cannot be 'sounded out', they believe they're stumped and may even resort to swinging a leg or biting a nail! No children should be restricted in this way.

> **All readers need a plan or strategy which they can follow when they don't recognize a word.**

Holdaway (1980) also refers to a 'central method of word attack'.

When word recognition is the problem, readers should:

---
a go back and read from the beginning of the sentence and/or read further on;
b check the first letter (or letter cluster);
c make a prediction (an informed guess!)

You, and the children, may be surprised at how often this strategy works! If it doesn't work, it may be appropriate to keep reading. However, if meaning is being lost, then the reader should seek help from someone else (teacher, parent, peer).

Common Materials/ Procedures and the Skills and Strategies they help to develop

Many materials and procedures in common use are valuable for supporting readers and helping them to learn essential reading skills and strategies. We have selected some commercially available materials in order to show how they lend themselves to certain procedures and to show how those procedures promote the development of reading skills and strategies. (Many other commercially available materials are equally useful, but only a small selection could be used as examples here.)

Material: 'Story Box' (Rigby)
Selection: *Mrs Wishy-washy* (a Read-Together book — Level 1)

Procedures:

a Shared-Book Experience

These 'Read-Together' books are intended mainly for shared-book experience and are first and foremost to be enjoyed. *Mrs Wishy-Washy* like the other 'Read-Together' books, has language which is highly predictable because the sentence patterns are repetitive, rhythm is used to advantage, and the illustrations support the text. Children are able to follow the story easily and naturally.

Shared-Book Experience actually includes several procedures: 'Discovery' and reading *to* children; 'Big Book' procedure; repeated readings; choral reading; and others. An excellent reference is Don Holdaway's book, *The Foundations of Literacy* (Ashton Scholastic, 1979).

b Oral Cloze

When reading the story to children, the teacher can stop at appropriate points in the text and have the children supply the next word or phrase. This develops children's prediction ability in particular and, as the teacher continues to read, the children also get immediate feedback about their attempts.

c Word Substitution

Children could be asked to replace the animals referred to in the text with different animals. New 'story' with same sentence patterns can be written up as a wall story. This reinforces the sentence patterns and extends vocabulary for all the children; for others it may also extend to word matching activities.

d Track and Cloze

Individual children in the group can take it in turns to use a pointer to follow under the text as the teacher reads it. When the teacher stops, the child following the text reads the next word or phrase. During this procedure, the teacher should encourage the children to test their predictions using graphophonic cues.

While the children are enjoying these books, they are also gaining essential understandings and learning important skills. Pages from 'The Story Box in the Classroom, Stage 1' are overleaf with annotations showing some of the understandings, skills and strategies children may be developing in addition to those mentioned above.

Mrs Wishy-washy (Read-together A)

Shared Reading

- Using the blown-up version, introduce Mrs Wishy-washy. Show the children the cover. Today's story is about Mrs Wishy-washy. What can you tell me about her? Why do you think she has her hands on her hips? I wonder who she is going to wash.

- Read the story adopting appropriate voices for the animals and a very bossy tone for Mrs Wishy-washy! If you have the cassette, listen to Step 1: Introduction and first reading

- At the end of the story, encourage impromptu responses and then ask questions. What happened? Were the animals naughty? Why? Was Mrs Wishy-washy bossy? What did she say?

- Point to the words Mrs Wishy-washy screamed ("Just look at you!") as you read them. Let the children practise their bossy voices. Explain that the exclamation mark tells you to scream too. Reread, inviting the children to join in.

- Practice the "wishy-washy" part.

Later Shared Readings
(Intersperse with related activities)

- Reread. Ask what each of the animals says ("Oh, lovely mud"). Divide the class into three groups. Practise saying the phrase in cow, duck, and pig voices. Reread together. Use Step 2 of the cassette in which music helps the children to read dramatically.

- Make up hand actions to follow the rhythm of "wishy-washy, wishy-washy" (e.g., shaking hands); "Oh, lovely mud" (e.g., clapping hands); and "Just look at you!" (e.g., wagging a finger). The children can do these actions as well as join in with the story. Step 3 of the cassette is excellent for this activity.

- Focus attention on the words spoken by Mrs Wishy-washy and the animals. Show the children the quotation marks and explain their function. See if they can find all the other direct speech in the book using this cue.
  Write out the direct speech on cards and let the children use these as they act out the story.

Annotations

Use of title and pictorial cues to make initial predictions and set purposes for reading.

Listening.

Initial responses; discussion (exchange and adaptation of ideas; new predictions).

Intonation/role play. Appropriate punctuation.

Focus on repeated words.

Dramatization; reading with expression.

Punctuation: quotation marks.

"In the tub you go."

In went the cow,
wishy-washy, wishy-washy.

In went the duck,
wishy-washy, wishy-washy.

'That's better,'
said Mrs Wishy-washy,

and she went into
the house.

"Oh lovely mud,"
they said.

- Dramatise. Four children can take the parts while the rest read-along and provide sound effects for "wishy-washy, wishy-washy" (e.g., rubbing hands together).

  Cards and acting to reinforce storyline and direct speech.

- Read-along at the listening post, using Step 4 of the cassette and multiple copies of the small version of the book.

  Dramatization
  Read-along
  both to develop familiarity with story.

Related Activities

- Children could write and draw about their favourite part, the whole story or one of the characters. Add a caption and ask the children about their picture.

  Expression of understanding through art or writing.

- Make a class version of the story by giving each child a copy of one page of the text. Using the original to copy from, if they wish, the children paint their version of each scene. As a group, put the book together, inviting the children to reconstruct the story in the correct sequence and then match with their pictures. Let them refer to the original if necessary. Hang the pages around the room as a wall story for about a week, then put them together as a big book.

  Plot; sequence of events.

- Innovate on the text by substituting different animals: "'Oh, lovely mud', said the *hippopotamus*, and he *wallowed* in it". Let the children draw a picture of the animal of their choice. Write the caption below, following the pattern of the original story. Put together as a class book.

  Focus on story structure; substitute different animals within same structure.

- Make a muddy mural. The background could be finger-painting. Each child could paint any big animal that loves mud, cut it out, and paste it on the background. Add the caption "Oh, lovely mud".

  Artistic expression.

- Get muddy. Let the children feel real mud squelch between their fingers and toes. Read the poem "Mud" on page 167 of *The Arbuthnot Anthology of Children's Literature*. Let them talk, write, and draw about their experience. Make a book.

  Sensual experience to extend understanding of and feeling for story. Related language activities. Related literature. Relating to own life experiences.

- Read other bathing stories to the children. *Mr Archimedes' Bath*, by P. Allen; *Time to Get out of the Bath*, *Shirley*, by J. Burningham.

- Talk about times when the children do naughty things when they are not being supervised by an adult.

- Read *The Wild Washerwoman*, by J. Yoeman and Q, Blake.

Material: 'Story Box' (Rigby)
Selection: *If you Meet A Dragon* (a Get-Ready book — Level 1)

The 'Get-Ready' books are used to introduce and reinforce very basic heavy duty words in the context of a story. All the titles repeat words many times, but because the repeated words are placed within a story with content words supported by illustrations, the children are able to use context cues from the outset. The text is *not* of the 'Oh oh oh, Jump jump jump' type. The Teachers' Manual points out that the children are not expected to read the content words without reference to the illustrations. '. . . any learning of these should be considered a bonus rather than an expectation.'

Procedures:

a Reading *to* children

Present the book; discuss title, covers and title page. Read the story joyfully or dramatically or quietly; however the story itself dictates. Allow children to join in as they recognize refrains or repetitive sentence patterns or story structure or illustrations.

b Cued Reading

Look at the book again; go through it and discuss pictures; re-tell in own words. Read book to children again, but use pointer to run along underneath the text. The children read along with the teacher as they are able. (This step is particularly helpful to the less confident reader.) The children learn directional conventions as the pointer moves and the pages are turned. (For some children, it may be useful to point to individual words to reinforce one-to-one correspondence.)

c Repeated Readings

The book is read whenever convenient. (Once only each time, but on different occasions; not several times in the one sitting.) If necessary, continue pointing. Children will use picture, semantic and syntactic cues more and more (it is not 'just memory').

d Dramatization

Whenever possible, teachers should read stories and let the children dramatize them. The dramatization allows the story to be expressed in new ways, it extends the text, and it adds new shades of meaning. It also adds to the repeated readings, but the time spent on a particular book is dictated by the children's continuing interest. Once group interest wanes, the teacher must move on, although individual children are given time every day to re-read favourite books.

e Word Masking

Word masking allows the teacher to focus attention on a particular word or word part so that 'heavy duty' words become sight words. It also allows the teacher to show children how affixes and inflectional endings can be added to the 'heavy duty' words to make related words (e.g. walk, walks, walked, walking; happy, unhappy). Masking is also necessary when the teacher wants to discuss some detail of print and have the children attend to the accompanying sound (the eye-ear link must be made in the earliest stages of reading).

f Cluster Analysis

Effective readers cluster letters into known chunks and break up unknown words in the same way. We can help all readers by helping them to respond to clusters within words. In the story. *If You Meet a Dragon*, the word 'tickle' is repeated several times. Using this as a target word, the cluster 'ick' can be studied. Choose three or four words containing 'ick' — for example: stick, tickle, quick. Follow these steps:

1) Teacher identifies word, the letters, and then the sound of the letter cluster.
   This word is 'stick'.
   We are looking at the cluster 'i-c-k' ('spell it out') which in this word stands for the sound /ick/.
2) Give the sound and ask for the letters which represent it.
   In the word 'stick', which letters stand for the /st/ sound? Which letters stand for the /ick/ sound?

3) Give the letters and ask for the sound in that word.

In the word stick, what sound do the letters 's-t-' stand for?

What sound do the letters 'i-c-k' stand for?

What is the whole word?

The intention is to help children with **whole word identification:** not to look at small details of print. Therefore, *whole* 'ick' words could be masked, but it is better *not* to mask the 'ick' part by itself because we want the children to be able to cluster while looking at whole words as they are reading.

The procedure is repeated for each of the three words. The time taken to do this is kept very short. Work quickly through each example; don't make each one an opportunity for a major recital. You could write the target word (tickle) and the other 'ick' words on the top of a chart which can then be added to over the next few days.

Clusters are usually at least three letters. Instead of studying 'i-e' words (there are too many of them anyway!) it is usually better to study 'ipe' words or 'ike' words.

A useful reference is Pulvertaft's book, *Carry On Reading* (Ashton Scholastic, 1978).

If You Meet a Dragon
(Get-ready A)

Shared Reading
- Discuss the picture on the cover. What do dragons do? What are those things on their back? What would you do if you met a dragon? Let's see what the children in the story do.

- Read the story with delight in your voice and great satisfaction at the end.

- Elicit a brief response. What did the children do? Was he a friendly dragon? Where did they tickle him? Did he like it? Do you like being tickled?

- *Reread*, doing one of the following each time:
  Point to the words as you go. Show the relationship between the content word and the picture. Which word says ''tickle''? Which says ''his''? Dramatise with one child as the dragon, one as the boy, and one as the girl. Use two scarfs to tickle the dragon.

Related Activities
- Sing ''Puff the Magic Dragon''.

- Read the poem ''Dinosaur'' on page 24 of *Tiddalik* (Story Box, Stage 7) to the children.

- Enjoy the poem, ''Grizzly Bear'' on page 127 of *The Arbuthnot Anthology of Children's Literature*.

- Read the story *The Bunyip from Berkeley's Creek*, by J. Wagner. Talk about what the children would do if they met the bunyip.

- (1) Children draw what they would do if they met a bunyip. Teacher asks about the picture and scribes the children's stories.

- (1) Children make a beautiful big dragon decorated with crepe paper twists. Have a scarf nearby so that the children can tickle the dragon. Write the text of the story underneath.

- (1) Children cut out the pictures on the stencil (page 153), then put them in sequence and retell the story in their own words. Let the children refer to the story if they need to.

Independent Reading
- (1) Add multiple copies of this title to the book box. Allow 5 to 10 minutes every day for independent rereading.

Material: 'Story Box' (Rigby)
Selection: 'Measles Are Very Catching' (from
'Sun Smile'. Stage 3)

Measles Are Very Catching
- Introduce this story as a shared book. Invite the children to join in with the repetitive parts, "Spots here, spots there, red spots were everywhere".

- Talk about illnesses that the children have had. Make a graph of the results. Get the children to illustrate.

- Make get-well cards for sick classmates and draw self-portraits of measles victims. At this age the children are familiar with the spots of measles, chicken pox, and German measles.

- Reread the story, making the following teaching points in context:
  — Compound words "Spots here, spots there, red spots were **every-where**" (page 31).
  — Find the word "**day**" (page 30). List other words that belong to the same word family; for example, "say", "play".

- Paint a picture of someone with the measles. Add captions. Make a mural from all the drawings of spotty faces. Add the caption "Spots here, spots there, red spots are everywhere".

The following selection from the teachers' manual also shows clearly how the 'Story Box' materials can be used to help children with reading skills.

Through the shared-book experience, the discussion about illnesses, the illustrations, and the mural with captions, children are given ample opportunity to express what they know and how they feel about measles, to extend their knowledge, to discover what experiences others have had and how they feel, to develop vocabulary, to develop concepts and understandings about health.

All of this is important in itself, but it is also giving the children opportunities to build the store of non-textual information which allows them to use the semantic cues within the text and to build language which allows them to use the syntactic cues within the text. Reading is not seen as an isolated, separate part of the day. It is part and parcel of much that happens in the room.

Through the reading or as a result of the reading, children will learn many of the skills they need. In this case, they may extend their knowledge and understanding about compound words or about 'ay' words.

However, the competent teacher must help them with other skills and must extend them or challenge them further so that new skills will be needed.

Material: Ginn Reading Program
Selection: *Baa Baa Black Sheep* (a 'Start With Rhymes' book, Level 1)

Procedures:

The procedures discussed by Johnson and Louis in *Literacy Through Literature* (Methuen, 1985) are particularly valuable. (See chapter 2 — 'Initial Instruction in Literacy'.)

Some of the procedures could be used with *Baa Baa Black Sheep* in the following ways:

a Shared Reading
The whole book of *Baa Baa Black Sheep* is shared; the teacher reads it with expression and interest. No attempt is made to isolate any of the language, but the teacher points to show directional convention. When the children read with the teacher, they must read with appropriate 'dramatic interpretation'. Using a felt board and cut-outs (a black sheep, 'three bags full', a master, a dame and a little boy) the teacher reads the story at every opportunity and encourages the children to join in.

b Word Masking
A word is covered and the children are asked to predict what it could be. For example:
Baa baa black_____
The word is uncovered and the children are asked, 'Were you right? Does that word say "sheep"? This has them focus on the word 'sheep' and helps to develop a sight vocabulary.

c Line framing
The children are presented with the full text in big print on the chalkboard or on a chart. After reading the whole text, whole lines can be 'framed' and the children are asked what that line says. There can be whole group responses, or volunteers can respond individually. Children who are able to frame lines themselves are given the opportunity to do so.

d Framing of familiar phrases and words. As above, but with phrases and words.

e Matching lines
The children match jumbled lines to the original complete text.

f Matching phrases
The text is cut into phrases. The teacher selects one phrase at a time and a child shows where it fits into the original.

Baa baa	black sheep

Have you any wool?

Yes sir, yes sir,	three bags full.

g Matching words
Use 'content' words (concrete nouns, action verbs, adjectives and adverbs) rather than 'function' words.

h Progressive cloze
The complete text is written on individual word cards.

Baa	baa	black	sheep	have	you	any
wool?						

Yes	sir	yes	sir,	three	bags	full.
One	for	the	master			
and	one	for	the	dame		
and	one	for	the	little	boy	
who	lives	down	the	lane.		

The text is read in unison and then individual content words are removed one or two at a time. The children re-read the rhyme, identifying the missing words. Structure words remain. (See Johnson and Louis, 1985. p.27.) The rhyme can be re-read as it is re-built.

i Lies

The complete text is available and read prior to this activity. The teacher presents:

Baa baa black *dog*

and says, 'It's supposed to say "Baa baa black sheep". Is anything wrong?' Volunteers name the incorrect word and give the correct one.

j Errors

The teacher presents:

Baa baa sack sheep
Have you any wood?
Yes sir, yes sir,
Tree bags full.

The teacher asks if anyone can see what is wrong. Volunteers point out the errors and correct them. The children are encouraged to verbalize their reasoning.

k Spoonerisms

These are fun and very useful for teaching phonics. The teacher presents:

One for the daster and one for the mame.

The children read what the line says and what it should say. They are encouraged to verbalize ('The 'd' and the 'm' are switched around; we need to take the 'd' off 'daster', the 'm' off 'mame', and then put them in the right spot.')

As Johnson and Louis point out, these 'play' activities with the language develop reading skills 'just as certainly (and more meaningfully) as the most analytically oriented phonics program'. (1985, p.36)

After completing the activities listed above for *Baa Baa Black Sheep*, the following skills will have been attended to:

Techniques	Skills Developed	
Words and phrases used: black sheep wool three bags full master dame little boy lives down the lane	Sight vocabulary	
Words predicted by the use of a mask: Baa Baa black sh_____ Have you any w_____ Yes sir, yes sir, three b_____full. One for the master and one for the dame And one for the l_____boy who l_____down the lane.	Use of context to predict appropriate word. Sound value of /sh/, /w/, /b/ and /l/. Sight vocab: sheep, went, bags, little, lives.	
Structure words highlighted in cloze activities: have, you, any, yes, for, the, and, who, down.	Sight vocab: high use structure words	
Lies Baa baa black dog. One for the little girl who lives down the street.	Sight vocab: dog/sheep girl/boy street/lane	
Errors Baa baa sack sheep Have you any wood? Yes sir, yes sir, Tree bags full.	Sound values: /s/ /bl/ /d/ /l/ /tr/ /thr/	Sight vocab: sack black wood wool tree three
Spoonerisms One for the daster and one for the mame.	Sound values: /d/ /m/ /m/ /d/	Sight vocab: master dame

References

Butler, A., *The Story Box in the Classroom —* Stage 1, Rigby, 1984.

——, *The Story Box in the Classroom —* Stages 2-7, Rigby, 1984.

Durkin, D., *Teaching Them To Read*, 2nd edn, Allyn & Bacon, 1974.

Pearson, P., & Johnson, D., *Teaching Reading Comprehension*, Holt, Rinehart and Winston, 1978.

10 THE LINKS BETWEEN READING AND WRITING

Introduction

The links between reading and writing are discussed more comprehensively in the companion volume, *Write On: A Conference Approach to Writing* (1985). The intention here is to briefly summarize the links that exist and make some further comments specifically about reading.

The links between reading and writing are as follows:

1 Writing and reading are both **constructive** processes.

The reader:	The writer:
reconstructs	**constructs**
another's	own
meaning	meaning
(comprehends)	(composes)

2 When writing or reading, construction of meaning or re-construction of another's meaning **develop and change.** It is commonly accepted that, during reading, comprehension develops and changes. It must also be accepted that the author's meaning is also developing and changing while writing (that meaning is not always clear before pen is put to paper).

3 Both writing and reading are processes which provide constant feedback and which require the writer or reader to make predictions. When writing, authors must read the text already generated and make predictions about what should come next.

4 Both writing and reading are **developmental** processes. Teachers must accept a child's initial attempts and gradual approximations towards conventionally correct forms of writing and reading. In this sense, the way we learn to write and read is no different from the way we learn other tasks.

Implications for Instructional Practice

Since reading and writing are in many ways interdependent, they should share many instructional practices.

It is obvious that children cannot write without reading, so while they are writing, they are learning much about reading. Even though children *can* read without having to write, their reading definitely teaches them much about writing. In fact, reading experience has a significant influence on writing ability. Stotsky (1983) reviewed the research and found that 'reading experience may be as critical a factor in developing writing ability as writing instruction itself'. Obviously, the quality of the reading program will have important effects on the way the children will write.

If the reading material that is available to the children in the reading program consists only of a highly restricted vocabulary or repeated sentence patterns of the 'I can . . .' type, then is it any wonder that teachers find that their children write with highly restricted vocabularies in boring 'I can . . .' stories?

Calkins has reported that 'the more children interact with their reading, the better they do in their writing.' (1983, p.158) She has also described classrooms where the questions asked during writing conferences are almost the same as those asked during reading conferences, a finding which is confirmed by many classroom teachers.

In her chapter titled 'Reading-Writing Connections', Calkins writes:

'I was wrong to view the two processes of reading and writing as separate. Wrong because writing involves reading, and because it reinforces and develops skills traditionally viewed as reading skills. And I was also wrong because writing can generate a stance toward reading which, regretfully, is rarely conveyed through reading programs.' (1983, p.155)

And later,

'Similarly, when children view themselves as authors, they approach texts with the consciousness of "I am one who needs to know how texts are made". Writing gives them a new reason to connect with reading.' (1983, p.157)

Many of the classroom teachers we work with have reported that, in time, the **writing and reading conferences become more and more alike.** That has also been our experience. Calkins reports similar findings, and lists some of the questions the children may be asking in reading conferences (1983, p.158).

These she notes, are almost the same as the questions the children may be asking in writing conferences.

Many classroom activities, such as 'wall stories' and 'shared book experience' help teachers to make points about both reading and writing. Whether the children are focussing on reading or writing, they will gain insights into both.

Children who are readers, write differently. Children who are writers, read differently.

Reading during the Writing Process

The following table shows how much reading may occur during any one writing session.

Writing	Reading opportunities and activities
Pre-writing (rehearsal)	– poetry reading – oral reading of stories in draft and published form – short story reading – play reading – activities such as extending children's sentences – cloze activities – 'read-a-long' taped stories
Writing	– children's oral reading of their drafts to selves and in conferences – silent reading during composition of drafts (to check meaning; to remind oneself of where the writing has been and where it should go; to regain momentum; to provide a 'breathing space' or even to avoid writing.) – researching books for material for stories – functional reading and the development of reference, library and study skills – reading aloud to check sense; to hear the 'sound' of the language.
Post-writing	– oral reading, first to publishing conference group, then for audience response – silent reading of own and other children's published stories – borrowing books from class and school libraries – choosing to read again a favourite book/story – reading and performance of plays written by children

Classroom Organization

The flowcharts for reading and writing are shown on facing pages so that the parallels are obvious.

The timetable teachers follow and the routines they set up can be similar for both the reading and writing sessions. The children are thus able to work within a predictable framework and the teacher can make expectations clear to all.

Reading

Interests; abilities; experiences; ideas; needs; aspirations; hobbies.

Perhaps I could / I need to read about that?

Shared Activities
Listening

Discussing

Attending to
a focus

- drawing
- note making
- skimming & browsing
- checking library
- active seeking
- establishing difficulty
- establishing appropriateness

Focus (usually teacher-planned)
- Sharing enthusiasms about books
- Sharing knowledge about authors
- Tr-reading — poetry; songs;
    — fiction/non-fiction
    — serial
- Teacher modelling

Reading
Emphasis on
- whole books
- real books
- silent reading
- understanding

- Setting purposes
- Comprehending
- Self-pacing in
    - interest
    - difficulty
    - speed
- Self-evaluation
    - personal satisfaction
    - skills
    - new interests
    - self-correction
    - future need

Conferences
- making connections
- establishing themes in literature
- discussion of content/message
- oral reading to establish facts, support points of view.
- re-construction of message (comprehension)
- attending to character, plot, setting, style, etc.

Teaching Groups
- skills practice
- oral reading; word identification; library skills; individual needs

Post-Reading Activities
- related reading
- creative response
    - writing
    - preparing for mime, drama, puppetry, etc.
    - art/craft
    - music
- audience reading

- study skills
    - topic studies
    - projects
    - research
- reading for life needs

Sharing
- choral reading
- performance
- debate
- display
- writing
- presentation of project of research
- interviewing

- discussion
    - insights
    - personal feelings
    - pleasure
    - empathy, etc.
- learning centres to support reading in content areas

Writing

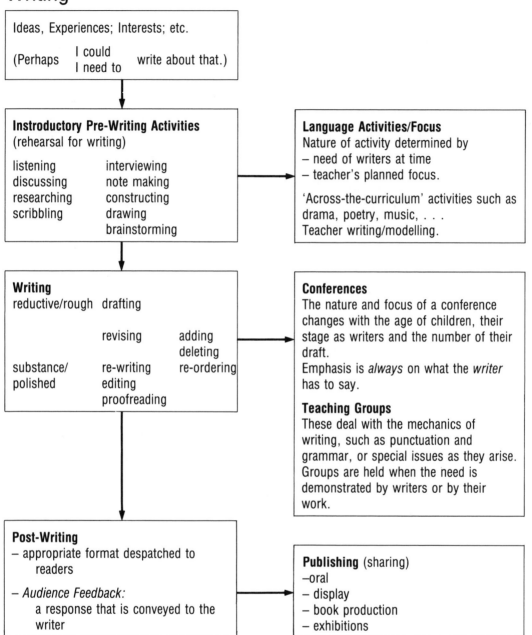

Ideas, Experiences; Interests; etc.

(Perhaps I could / I need to write about that.)

Instroductory Pre-Writing Activities
(rehearsal for writing)

listening   interviewing
discussing   note making
researching   constructing
scribbling   drawing
                   brainstorming

Language Activities/Focus
Nature of activity determined by
– need of writers at time
– teacher's planned focus.

'Across-the-curriculum' activities such as
drama, poetry, music, . . .
Teacher writing/modelling.

Writing
reductive/rough   drafting

                  revising   adding
                                  deleting
substance/   re-writing   re-ordering
polished   editing
                  proofreading

Conferences
The nature and focus of a conference
changes with the age of children, their
stage as writers and the number of their
draft.
Emphasis is *always* on what the *writer*
has to say.

Teaching Groups
These deal with the mechanics of
writing, such as punctuation and
grammar, or special issues as they arise.
Groups are held when the need is
demonstrated by writers or by their
work.

Post-Writing
– appropriate format despatched to
  readers

– *Audience Feedback:*
  a response that is conveyed to the
  writer

Publishing (sharing)
–oral
– display
– book production
– exhibitions

This process is recursive, not linear.

The 'pattern' for each session is as follows:
- whole class together
- individual and group activities
- whole class together again.

During the reading session there will always be time for silent reading (sometimes called Uninterrupted Sustained Silent Reading). Occasionally, during the writing session, it is also appropriate to include time for silent writing in a diary or journal (which could be called Uninterrupted Sustained Silent Writing!)

Parallel programs allow for children to attend to both reading and writing in either or both sessions — whole language learning is the key.

References

Carlkins, L., *Lessons from a Child*, Heinemann, 1983.

Harste, J., Woodward, V. & Burke, C., *Language Stories and Literacy Lessons*, Heinemann Educational Books, 1984.

Holt, S. & Vacca, J., 'Reading with a Sense of Writer: Writing with a Sense of Reader', *Language Arts*, 58, 8, 1981, p. 937.

Hopkins, H., *From Talkers to Readers the Natural Way*, Ashton Scholastic, 1977.

Parry, J. & Hornsby, D., *Write On: A Conference Approach to Writing*, Martin Educational, 1985.

Shanklin, N., 'Relating Reading and Writing: Developing a Transactional Theory of the Writing Process', monograph in Language and Reading Studies, School of Education, Indiana University, 1981.

Stotsky, S., 'Research on Reading/Writing Relationships: a synthesis and suggested directions', *Language Arts* 60, 5, 1983, p. 677.

Turbill, J. & Butler, A., *Towards a Reading/Writing Classroom*, Primary English Teaching Association, 1984.

11 READING ALOUD TO CHILDREN

The Importance of Reading Aloud to Children

Children do not learn to enjoy reading unless they are read to. They cannot know what reading *is* unless they are read to. Reading to children provokes their curiosity and arouses their desire to *want* to read.

Since two essential prerequisites for learning to read are the desire to do so and an understanding of what reading is, we can understand why it is so important to read to children.

The experience of teachers and parents and the findings of much research have also shown the importance of reading to children. The absolute necessity of reading to children (at all levels) is beyond debate. In addition to helping children acquire essential prerequisites for learning to read, reading aloud to children also stirs imaginations, improves general language skills, expands vocabulary, improves classroom atmosphere and maintains positive attitudes to reading. Furthermore, good oral reading helps to develop a taste for the best in children's literature.

Oral reading to children introduces them to the different *sounds* of language. They need to *hear* the RAAF-type language in *Closer to the Stars* (Max Fatchen); the desperate language in *Once There Was a Swagman* (Hesba Brinsmead) when Teddy, lost in the bush, suddenly steps on nothing and falls through blackness, hits rocks and then slides helplessly into icy water which knocks the breath from her lungs. They need to *hear* the tongue-twisting language of *Tikki Tikki Tembo* and the slow but steady language of the tortoise in *The Hare and the Tortoise*. They need to hear the loud, angry language of the dragon Smaug in *The Hobbit* (J.R.R. Tolkien) and the soft, pitiful voice of *The Little Matchgirl* (Hans Christian Andersen) or the whisper in *Some One* (Walter de la Mare). They need to hear the language of

nonsense in some of the *Mother Goose* rhymes or works by Edward Lear.

Another reason why teachers and parents should read aloud to children is that, very often, the children's skill in reading is insufficient to enable them to read books in which they are interested. We can acknowledge their interests, read to them, and get them 'hooked on books'.

But one of the most important reasons for reading aloud to children is that by doing so, we can share with them **literature which extends their thinking.** For younger children in particular, the material they are able to read themselves may not provide the mental challenge they are capable of meeting. Even 11- and12-year-olds may find much literature too difficult to understand or appreciate fully if they are required to read it on their own. However, if this literature is read aloud to them, they may be able to respond to it with a deeper level of understanding. A reading/literature program must therefore provide both listening and silent reading opportunities for children.

Reading Aloud and Silent Reading: Natural Partners

We have described reading sessions in which a period of silent reading is always included. Sustained silent reading (or quiet enjoyment of books even from the first day of school) is essential. Trelease (1984) describes classrooms where sustained silent reading by the children and reading aloud by the teacher are everyday features. In these classrooms, the children are enthusiastic about books and excited by them.

We have also been keen participators in classrooms such as these where reading is seen to be a form of recreation, and yet serious reading skills and strategies are being learned and used.

The *Read-Aloud Handbook* by Trelease is an excellent paperback reference for both teachers and parents. It includes chapters on when to begin reading aloud to children, the stages of reading aloud, and the do's and don'ts of reading aloud. The second half of the book is called 'A Treasury of Read-Alouds' and contains a listing of books that have a 'proven track record of success' as read-alouds. Each title listed has an accompanying synopsis, other read-alouds by the same author and related titles. The Treasury is divided into six categories: wordless books, picture books, short novels and stories for younger listeners, novels, anthologies and poetry.

For the teacher who wishes to read aloud to children every day, other useful references are: Hearne (1981) and Huck (1979).

In addition, we have included a list of 'Sure Fire Winners' at the end of this chapter.

Read Aloud Daily

We must read aloud to children every day.

> 'It can be done. Whether you are a teacher or a parent, don't tell me there isn't enough time — we find time for what we value.' (Trelease, 1984, p.32)

Trelease has discovered, as have many teachers and parents, that reading to children is a wondrous experience which costs only time and interest. He promises that, once started, you will never want the experience to end.

> 'My children and I have sat in a one-room schoolhouse with Carol Ryrie Brink's *Caddie Woodlawn*, chased monsters with Maurice Sendak and Mercer Mayer, . . . and swallowed magic potions with Judy Blume in *Freckle Juice*. With *James and the Giant Peach* by Roald Dahl, we crossed the shark-infested waters of the North Atlantic; we battled a Caribbean hurricane in Theodore Taylor's *The Cay*. We have searched for wayward brothers and sisters, evaded wolves, lost friends, and learned how to make new ones. We have laughed, cried, shaken with fright, and shivered with delight. And, best of all, we did it together.

Along the way we discovered something about the universality of human experience — that we, too, have many of the hopes and fears of the people we read about.' (1984, p.22)

Listening and Responding

Usually, when a teacher reads to children, the only response sought is a spontaneous and personal one. Children should be given opportunities to simply listen to, and enjoy, good literature. However, encouraging certain responses sometimes helps children to gain a deeper understanding and appreciation of what is being read. Some books invite particular responses. Even so, most activities following oral reading to the class should be kept short and to the point. Some will develop over time as a book is read as a serial (e.g., making of a mural). But *all* activities must increase the children's involvement with the book.

The *reading* is the most important activity; follow-up activities must never be drawn out and boring or the children will tend to view them as a punishment for listening!

Suggested Activities

Discussion

Children should always have the opportunity to spend some time discussing a selection after it has been read to them. This does **not** have to be a whole-class discussion; it can often be handled best by letting small groups (of three or four at the most) sit together for a discussion. Some children may prefer to spend a few minutes quickly drawing their impression of what was read.

Consensus Activities

After listening to a chapter (or relevant section) the children jot down what they think are the most important points for that chapter. Then, in small groups of two or three, they have one minute each to *justify* or *clarify* their points. After that time, the children can amend or re-order their points if necessary.

This activity can be extended by bringing the whole class together and reaching a consensus about a class list of the most significant events or issues in that chapter (or section). This list can be recorded on a chart. The charts can then be bound to make a class book.

Listing and classifying

After a chapter or section has been read, the listing and classifying activities can be done individually, in groups or even as a whole class. Remember, these and similar activities should take only a few minutes (they should be 'short and sharp').

Characters	Events
Fudge	wouldn't eat
Father	tipped food over Fudge
Peter	got dog

People	Places	Things

Character	Describing words

Good	Bad

These activities provide structures and language for remembering the story while it is being read. They help to structure thought and clarify concepts, which in turn help children to verbalize their understanding and appreciation of the story.

These activities also extend vocabulary and help the children to see how authors use words.

Mainly Maps!

1 Tracing journeys on large maps; finding actual places in an atlas.
   e.g. *Walkabout* by James Vance Marshall (Australia)
   I Am David by Ann Holmes   (Europe)
   The Silver Sword by Ian Serraillier (Europe)

2 Draw plan of story setting.
   e.g. *Granny Stickleback* by John Moore
   Plan showing places where children are kidnapped.

3 Marking places/events on maps provided.
   e.g. *The Hobbit* by J.R.R. Tolkien
   The Riddle of the Trumpalar by Judy Bernard-Waite

4 Make comic strips to show story sequence.
   e.g. *The Iron Man* by Ted Hughes
   Run For Your Life by David Line
   Children could work in pairs for this kind of activity. It is usually best done at the end of each chapter/section.

Art/Craft

There are many art/craft activities which could accompany or follow oral reading to a whole class and other references should be consulted. Again, the *reading* itself is the most important activity. Children should be able to choose individually whether they do the art/craft activities or not. Many will be co-operative endeavours, several children being involved, as for example with painting a mural or erecting a large display.

1 Make clay or plasticine models of characters from:
  e.g. *Finn Family Moomintroll* by Tove Jansson and other Moomintroll books;
  Mrs Pepperpot books by Alf Proysen;
  Wombles in Danger by Elizabeth Beresford.

2 Make puppets. Some can be quite simple; others quite sophisticated.
  e.g. *Mrs Frisby and the Rats of NIMH* by Robert O'Brien
    — sock puppets
  The Worst Witch by Jill Murphy
    — shadow puppets

3 Dioramas
  Again, these will usually be constructed by groups of children.
  e.g. *The Hills of the Black Cockatoo* by Pat Peatfield Price
    — outback Australia scene

4 Models
  e.g. The 'Green Knowe' house (books by Lucy Boston)
  The raft from *Adrift* by Allan Baillie
  One (or several) of the houses from *A House is a House For Me* by Mary Ann Hoberman
  Tilly's 'Zoom Broom' from *Space Witch* by Don Freeman

5 Special Paint Effects.
  e.g. Marbling — as background for black ink silhouettes in the style of Jan Pienkowski's illustrations for many of Joan Aitken's short stories.

6 Threads and Textiles.
  e.g. Make a web for Charlotte (*Charlotte's Web* by E.B. White)
  Make a clothesline with miniature clothes after reading *Mrs Mopple's Washing Line* by Anita Hewett.

7 Mobiles.
  e.g. Make a mobile of all the items picked up and blown by the wind in *The Wind Blew* by Pat Hutchins.
  Make a mobile of some event from *Flat Stanley* by Jeff Brown.

8 Murals.
  e.g. Group painting of a mural which depicts all the animals (in sequence) from *A Fly Went By* by Mike McClintock.

Activities are fun because they give you a rest from reading for a while and when you do questions it makes you realise more things about the book.

Tabitha

Drama

1 Mime
  e.g. *Amelia Bedelia* by Peggy Parish. Mime one of Amelia's disasters on the job; others guess.

2 Acting
  e.g. *The Great Big Enormous Turnip.* Children act out story.
  For older children, acting out a short scene from a book like *Chase Through the Night* by Max Fatchen can be an enjoyable and valuable learning experience.

3 Role Playing
  e.g. *Tales of a Fourth Grade Nothing* by Judy Blume.
  Children assume roles of Peter and Fudge in a situation from the story.

Sure-Fire Winners

Only the teacher, who knows the children well, can select appropriate books to read aloud. However, the titles listed below have been most successful when read to many classes. There is no such thing as a book for Year 2 children or for Year 6 children, so year levels have not been included with the list. However, there has been an attempt to list the 'easiest' books first and the 'hardest' ones last. Teachers who know their children and know literature will be able to make appropriate decisions. Many references are available to help teachers make these decisions.

The Three Billy Goats Gruff and other folk-tales of challenge and achievement.
The Tale of Peter Rabbit (Beatrix Potter)
The Very Hungry Caterpillar (Eric Carle)
Millions of Cats (Wanda Gag)
Clever Polly and the Stupid Wolf (Catherine Storr)
Little Old Mrs Pepperpot (Alf Proysen)
Fantastic Mr Fox (Roald Dahl)
The Muddle-headed Wombat (Ruth Park)
Caps For Sale (Esphyr Slobodkina)
Where the Wild Things Are (Maurice Sendak)
Alexander and the Terrible, Horrible, No Good, Very Bad Day (Judith Viorst)
Charlotte's Web (E.B. White)
Green Smoke (Rosemary Manning)
The Midnight Fox (Betsy Byars)
The Eighteenth Emergency (Betsy Byars)
The Iron Man (Ted Hughes)
The Great Piratical Rumbustification (Margaret Mahy)
The Librarian and the Robbers (Margaret Mahy)
James and the Giant Peach (Roald Dahl)
The Mousewife (Rumer Godden)
The Lion, The Witch, and The Wardrobe (C.S. Lewis)
Mrs Frisby and the Rats of Nimh (Robert O'Brien)
A Wrinkle in Time (Madeleine L'Engle)
Bridge to Terabithia (Katherine Paterson)
The Silver Sword (Ian Serraillier)
I Am David (Anne Holm)
The Phantom Tollbooth (Norton Juster)
Tuck Everlasting (Natalie Babbitt)
Run For Your Life (David Line)
Sounder (William Armstrong)
Hating Alison Ashley (Robin Klein)
The Cats (Joan Phipson)
The Seventh Pebble (Eleanor Spence)
The Hobbit (J.R.R. Tolkien)
The Wolves of Willoughby Chase (Joan Aiken)
Chanticleer and the Fox (Barbara Cooney)
The Dark is Rising (Susan Cooper)
A Wizard of Earthsea (Ursula Le Guin)
The Witch of Blackbird Pond (Elizabeth George Speare)

Reading Traditional Literature to Children

Traditional literature, which includes folk tales, fables, myths, legends and epics, helps children to understand all literature. Huck (1979) writes that it helps them to build 'a framework for literature' as they meet again and again the themes of saviour heroes, cruel stepmothers, the cycle of seasons, the cycle of man's life, and so on. Much of our present vocabulary comes from traditional literature; 'titanic' comes from the powerful Titans; 'panic' from the god Pan; 'cereal' from Ceres the grain goddess. And we have such phrases as 'sour grapes' and 'boy who cried wolf' from traditional literature.

Folk tales are familiar and probably the most appealing. Modern illustrated versions are appropriate even for the youngest primary school children. Folk tales are usually short, simple stories which children often label as 'make believe'. Fables are also short, but they are sometimes highly complex stories and are usually suitable only for middle primary and older children. The most common are the fables of Aesop and La Fontaine.

Myths are generally about gods and the creation of things; they are about good and evil. They are good stories, packed with action and conflict. However, they are complicated by complex symbolism and unfamiliar language, and are not generally appropriate until the upper primary level. But they *must* be read to children. They have imaginative qualities which enchant children and suspense which enthrals them. Suitable versions must be selected and it would be wise to consult a librarian. We would advise that you obtain those by outstanding authors such as Leon Garfield, Robert Graves, Ian Serraillier and Rosemary Sutcliff.

Legends are often grouped with myths. They are described by Huck (1979) as 'stories about heroes and their mighty deeds before the time of recorded history'. Again, suitable versions must be found.

Epics are generally considered to be a 'cycle of tales' about one human hero. They developed from the myths and legends. Earlier epics, such as the *Iliad* and the *Odyssey* still have gods intervening, but the focus shifts from the gods to a human hero, such as Beowulf, King Arthur or Robin Hood. The hero embodies the ideals of a culture. 'Both King Arthur and Robin Hood appealed to the English love of justice and freedom; King Arthur and his knights represented the code of chivalry, while Robin Hood was the champion of the common man.' (Huck, 1979, p.222) Epics contribute to an understanding of the highest moral values of a society.

Specific incidents from the *Iliad* (such as the Trojan Horse) and from the *Odyssey* (such as the horrifying experience with the one-eyed cyclops) will hold children spellbound.

The Bible is also part of traditional literature. 'It makes little sense to tell children the story of Jack the Giant Killer but to deny them the stories about David and Goliath or Samson.

They read of the wanderings of Ulysses, but not those of Moses.' (Huck, 1979, p.228) Many picture-story books of separate stories are available, including those by Walter de la Mare, Beatrice De Regniers and Brian Wildsmith.

References

Education Department of Victoria, *Happily Ever After*, 1975

Hearne, B., *Choosing Books for Children*, Dell Publishing Co., 1981.

Huck, C., *Children's Literature in the Elementary School*, 3rd edn. updated, Holt, Rinehart and Winston, 1979.

Sutherland, Z. & Arbuthnot, M., *Children and Books*, 5th edn, Scott Foresman, 1977.

Trelease, J., *The Read-Aloud Handbook*, Penguin, 1984.

Evaluation and the Teaching/Learning Program

Record keeping and evaluation are part of a total program; they are not separate issues. Consequently, record keeping and evaluation decisions will vary depending on school policy and program. There can be no blueprint presented in this chapter. However, given certain beliefs about developmental learning, about the reading process and about how children best learn to read, then *evaluation of individual children ought to be a natural phenomenon in every classroom every day*. Evaluation should not be seen as a separate issue; it is an integral part of the teaching/learning program. When educators divorce evaluation from the rest of the program, it becomes purposeless. It becomes evaluation for evaluation's sake. It becomes 'the evaluation problem'. Then educators look for universal remedies or bold new approaches. Finding neither, they return to regurgitations of statements about testing. They get caught up in the illusion of numbers which seem to have statistical validity and the divorce is complete. They fail to remember that evaluation is much broader than mere measurement of a few relatively trivial aspects of reading. (Perhaps they also fail to understand that the trivial 'surface features' measured do not constitute reading.

Many of the most important aspects of all learning cannot be tested or measured.

'In any "subject", if the emphasis is on process rather than content, on understanding rather than mind-stocking, on application of knowledge to new situations rather than parroting snippets of information, then evaluation is difficult . . . Content is reasonably easy to teach and learn — recall reasonably easy to test. Understanding is much more difficult to teach, learn and test. The difficulty exists in all "subjects" . . .
Primary education is now concerned with individual development in a social context rather than with subject performance . . . Consequently *evaluation* is more concerned with what children can *do* than with what they *know*. (Note, however, that they utilise knowledge in actions.) Evaluation concentrates on seeking out and developing pupil potential rather than on grading, selecting and predicting. It also examines our contribution as teachers and the material of the course of study we present.'
Vaughan, J. (formerly Assistant Director-General of Education, N.S.W. Education Department) in '101 Questions Primary Teachers Ask', P.E.T.A., 1980, pp.192-3.

Program Evaluation

When evaluation is part of the total program, it is followed by changing, where necessary, methods and materials.

The evaluation of the program should start with asking questions about current practices. A useful reference is *Reading On* (Gilmour & Tyrer, 1985, chapter 6). It suggests questions such as:

- What are the reasons for the particular activities your children are engaged in throughout the school day?
- What are the reasons for the particular activities being included?

- What are the children gaining from these activities?
- Are the outcomes of these activities in line with school policy?
- What resources are available?

Evaluation should also take into account the various strands of the reading program (see chapter 3) and ensure that a balance has been achieved.

Standardized Testing

> It is not appropriate to use group standardized tests to evaluate an individual child's progress, or to group children for teaching purposes.

The purpose of standardized, norm-referenced tests has often been misunderstood. (See Gilmour & Tyrer, 1985, p. 63.) *Such tests do **not** evaluate individual performance. They do not tell a teacher where to start teaching.* Standardized tests, if used at all, can only be used to describe limited aspects of the performance of a large group. In addition, the test should only be used to judge the group's performance with the reference or norm group *if the groups are comparable.* It is very difficult to find tests that have norm groups with which valid comparisons can be made (and the interpretation of scores is misleading if the norming population differs from the pupil population, which is usually the case).

Educational literature on evaluation has many warnings about the use of standardized tests. The reading abilities sampled are limited (Strang, 1968); many are not valid since they do not test what they claim to be testing (Tuinman, 1973); in comprehension of paragraphs, the subjects often know the point of the testing before they read the paragraph (Pyrczak, 1972); in multiple choice questions, clues within the questions themselves often give away many of the answers (Weaver and Bickely, 1967); intelligence tests and reading tests often have a section called 'vocabulary' but the tasks are radically different (MacGinitie, 1973); most word recognition sub-tests evaluate spelling ability rather than reading ability (Winkley, 1971). The list could go on and on.

Obviously, standardized norm-referenced tests have to be considered carefully before they are used. The user *must* be able to answer the following questions:

1 What is the purpose of using the test?
2 Does the test match *my* objectives?
3 Is the test valid (does it measure what it is supposed to measure)?
4 Is the group I am going to test comparable to the norm group?
5 What will it tell me that I don't already know?
6 What will it tell me that I can't find out in other ways?

Student Evaluation

> Evaluation must focus on individuals and encourage development rather than competition.

Current literature available on evaluation strongly supports a focus on individuals and their own progress (that is, their performance now compared with their performance at an earlier time).

'In seeking to ensure success for all students, schools should:
(a) provide a caring and supportive environment;
(b) ensure that students are clear about what they are expected to accomplish and provide them with increasing opportunities to help determine the educational tasks and goals that are set for them;
(c) base assessment of students' work on their success in reaching achievable goals; and
(d) ensure that assessment policies do not emphasise comparisons between students and that the reporting of student progress to students, parents and prospective employers focuses on what students have achieved and on their developing talents and competencies.'
Ministerial Paper No. 6,
'Curriculum Development and Planning in Victoria', 1984, p.14, 9.8.

'Evaluation processes will be through descriptive assessment and individualised diagnostic profiles. These methods will record developments in other than norm-referenced ways . . .'
Victorian Education Department, submission to Basic Learning in Primary Schools Program, May 1985.

This is also true at the post-primary level. The following quotes come from 'Assessment in English: Years 7 – 10' (Education Department of Victoria, 1982).

'To place high value upon comparisons among children and upon competition is to deny natural development and to close off possibilities for growth in language and thought.' (p.8)
'Measurement, in quantifiable terms, is not an appropriate concept for many facets of English because much of English curriculum cannot be reduced to easily and objectively measurable criteria.' (p.9)
'Growth (in language) is best assessed in carefully formulated, descriptive, nongraded, noncompetitive terms.' (p.10)

The individualized, literature-based program described in this text has many 'in-built' features which allow for the evaluation of individual children. The evaluation is structured and systematic. It is based on purposeful record keeping and individual evaluation procedures which encourage development.

Evaluation from Records Kept

Records are kept as a result of the careful and systematic observation of the children's use of language (listening, speaking, reading and writing).

It is essential to keep meaningful and adequate records, as it is impossible to evaluate without them. However, record keeping is not evaluation. Evaluation requires the teacher and the children to go *beyond* the records kept. It requires the teacher to make *judgements* about each child's growth and development. Evaluation may also require the use of some procedures that will help teachers obtain more detailed diagnostic information for individual children.

Records are not kept unless they have a specific purpose. We should only record what is useful. Records are useful if they help teachers evaluate individual children; if they help children make self-evaluations; if they help teachers to improve their programs and their teaching; if they help teachers communicate with parents and administrators.

Records should be used to compare a child's performance with his or her *own* previous performance, never to compare children competitively or to label or grade them. In such comparative labelling there is the danger of lowering the teacher's expectations of what a child can achieve and of lowering the child's view of him/herself as a learner.

Teacher's Records and Evaluation

Record: Weekly Program

The Weekly Program records:
- conferences
- teaching groups
- share time participants
- notes about children to check
- development of introductory activities

Evaluation:
The records kept in the teacher's weekly program provide useful and accessible information about how children are working within the reading program. The teacher can quickly scan these records, weekly or fortnightly, to see which children may need encouragement and support or an invitation to participate in small group procedures operating within the room.

Record: Individual Conference Log

During an individual conference, teachers will be able to identify and record many aspects of reading that they wish to evaluate, including
- attitude
- participation
- selection skills
- comprehension
- oral reading ('running records')
- use of textual cues
- word identification strategies

Evaluation:
The records made during the individual conference are perhaps the most significant of all the teacher's records and are essential to an adequate evaluation of children. The individual conference allows the teacher to closely observe many reading behaviours, understandings, attitudes and skills.

Over significant periods of time, changes can show where there have been developments. It is also necessary to determine where no development has occurred so that future planning is purposeful.

Teachers may find the 'Reading Record' sheets useful as a 'checklist' for the reading behaviours, skills and attitudes that must be evaluated. Detailed guidance is also available in Don Holdaway's book, *Independence In Reading*, 1980 (Appendix C — 'A Simplified Progression of Word Recognition Skills' and Appendix D — 'Sequential Development of Reading Skills').

It is during the individual conference that teachers may require the child to read orally. This provides an opportunity to keep 'running records' of oral reading. This could include miscues, intonation, appropriate pausing, articulation, pace, ability to look up from the text and back again, and significant aspects of oral reading performance.

Comments may also be recorded about the child's selection skills, written work, reading in the content areas, use of reference materials and results of child self-evaluations.

The information in the Log should also be shared with the child, who can discover what advances have been made over time.

Record: Interest Inventory

This helps the teacher to provide reading materials that might be appropriate, especially at the beginning of the year, and to make some early indications of the children's attitudes to reading. (See Appendix 1)

Evaluation:

Although the Interest Inventory is most useful at the beginning of the year to help with planning of materials for the program, it also allows monitoring, over time, to ascertain whether readers' interests have broadened as a result of the program.

Record: Reading Interview

The Reading Interview (C. Burke, 1977) is useful for the teacher of children who are having difficulties.

Evaluation:

The interview helps to determine which model of reading/language-learning the child uses and his or her reading strategies. It gives the teacher specific information upon which to act.

Record: Reading Attitude Scales

Several scales for determining reading attitudes exist. *The Carter Attitude to Reading Scales* (C.A.R.S.) is useful and looks at attitudes to reading at school, at home and in the library. (Ref: Riverina C.A.E., 1978)

Evaluation:

Initial results from attitude scales can be used to evaluate children's attitudes and to make necessary decisions about priorities in the program. Over significant periods of time, they can also be used to monitor *changes* in attitudes. If attitudes become more positive, this provides important information not only about the program but also about the child's approach to reading.

Children's Records and Evaluation

Record: Reading Folder
(see chapter 4)

1 'Titles I Would Like To Read' — inside front cover.

This is a list which children add to as their interests expand and as they come to know more books.

2 'Conference Record' — inside back cover.

This is a record of when conferences have been held and why they were held.

3 'Books I've Read' — sheet inside folder.

This is a list of titles read. Starting and finishing dates are included. (Individual teachers will need to decide exactly which books are recorded here. It is sometimes appropriate to record *all* books read; it may only be appropriate to record self-chosen books; it may include material prescribed by the teacher, such as graded (but literature-based!) material. The decision about what is to be recorded is based on the *purpose* of keeping such a record.

4 'Activity Record' — sheet inside folder.

This is a list of all activities completed. It shows the children and the teacher if there is variety in the activities completed.

Evaluation:

When children are keeping their own folder records, the teacher is able to evaluate their record keeping abilities and their attention to the task of record keeping. Children must come to see that such record keeping *is* important and must develop a positive attitude towards it.

Each of the reading folder records helps to determine how the child is working within the program and helps the teacher to decide where encouragement or direction is required. The list of 'Titles I Would Like To Read' can indicate a growing expansion of interests and a changing attitude to reading. The 'Conference Record' indicates the child's attendance at both individual and group conferences and his or her reasons for attending conferences.

(Is the child attending conferences often enough? Does the child know when to ask for a conference? Is the child able to state why he or she needs a conference?)

The list of 'Books I've Read' helps the teacher to monitor the choices the child is making and whether or not the child is reading a wide range of materials for different purposes. It indicates whether or not the child is reading different genres and different authors. It gives an indication of how many books are being read (although the record may not include everything read). The 'Activity Record' helps the teacher to make judgements about a child's responses to reading and whether or not the child is able to respond in a variety of ways. Responding through activities may also be an indication of what impact books are having on the child.

Record: Reading Log:

- 'Required comments' are entered in this book.
- The title of the book is used as the heading.
- The author and the illustrator are recorded.
- The child's own comment about the book is written.
- The child may illustrate entry.

Lower grades:
- Written responses and illustrations can be recorded on sheets of paper that the children normally write on; these can be stapled into a book.
- Written response may simply be the name of a favourite character, or a special word.

READING RECKONER		Read by
Title/Author		D.C C.N. DH D.M. D.W. KG
The Turbulent Term of Tyke Tyler	Gene Kemp	D.C C.N. DH D.M. D.W. KG
The Wolves of Willoughby Chase	Joan Aiken	J.H. G.D. D.W D.C. D.H. K.G
Superfudge	Judy Blume	B.H. M.F. B.D. D.M. M.B. K.G.
Five Children and It	E. Nesbit	D.W. D.M. D.C. J.H. B.D. C.N.
Fantastic Mr. Fox	Roald Dahl	B.D. G.D. J.H. K.G. B.H. K.G
The Trouble with Donovan Croft	Bernard Ashley	D.M D.W. C.N. D.W. M.B. J.H
Under the Mountain	Maurice Gee	B.D. D.M C.N. D.C. M.F. KG.
Collins Guide to Dinosaurs	David Lambert	D.W. B.H. DM C.N. D.C. G.D.

Evaluation:

Over a period of time, teachers can go through children's reading books and identify development in the following broad areas:

1 specific recognition and recall from memory (literal comprehension)
2 ability to re-organize ideas and information (re-organization)
3 ability to form hypotheses based on ideas stated and on personal experiences (inferential comprehension)
4 ability to make judgements (evaluation)
5 ability to make personal responses (appreciation)

Over time, the child's ability to write the required comments can also be monitored. This might include the use of 'guiding questions', ability to write comments without the guiding questions and whether or not written work receives thoughtful consideration.

Record: Self-evaluation Form
('Am I Developing as an Independent Reader?')

This is a reproducible page (see Appendix 1).
The form should be adapted for use with children of different ages or children with different experiences in self-evaluation. The completion of this form by the child is a valuable learning experience in itself.

Children will need guidance when first making entries; *teachers need to help them know about reading and what their individual goals might be.*

Completing this form helps students become 'clear about what they are expected to accomplish' and provides them with 'increasing opportunities to help determine the educational tasks and goals that are set for them'. (Ministerial Paper 6, 1984, p.14)

Class Records and Evaluation

The following class records help the teacher and the children to evaluate the reading **program.** They do not indicate anything about individual children.

Reading Reckoner

a This is simply a growing list of all titles read.
b It is best if displayed on a large chart for everyone to see.
c It shows the children that they *are* readers.
d It directs children to others who have read the same title.
e It shows the children the variety of reading material they have chosen.
f It helps in organizing group conferences.

READING RECKONER

Author/Title	Name
James and the Giant Peach -Roald Dahl	Deanne Cannan
Helen Keller - M. Davidson	Christine N.
Unspun Socks from a Chicken's Laundry - S. Milligan	Debbie M.
The Cay - Theodore Taylor	Debbie M.
The Nimbin - J. Wagner	Brendan D.
The Hobbit - J. R. Tolkien	Dean W.
Storm Boy - Colin Thiele	Michelle F.
The Silver Chair - C.S. Lewis	David W.
Black Dog - C. Mattingley	Brenton H.
Treasure Island - R.L. Stevenson	Glenn D.
Great Gorillas - A. McGovern	Dean W.
Easy Magic For Beginners -R. Brackel	Michelle B.
Now We Are Six - A.A. Milne	Kristi G.
I Own The Racecourse -P. Wrightson	Jackie H.

Lists of selected books, authors, poets and illustrators enjoyed

These lists should be constantly reviewed.

Example from Year 1/2

Favourite Illustrators — Term 1

David McKee	I Hate My Teddy Bear King Rollo and New Shoes
Stan & Jan Berenstain	Bears in the Night
Quentin Blake	The Enormous Crocodile
Jenny Wagner	John Brown, Rose and the Midnight Cat
Jan Pienkowski	Meg and Mog books
Ezra Jack Keats	The Trip
Beatrix Potter	The Tale of Peter Rabbit
Maurice Sendak	Where the Wild Things Are
Eric Hill	Spot's First Walk Where's Spot
Yasuo Ohtomo	Ready, Steady, Go! How Do I Eat? Hallo! How Are You?

Example from Year 5:

Favourite Authors — Term 2

Roald Dahl	The Twits The BFG George's Marvellous Medicine
Michael Rosen	Quick, Let's Get Out of Here Mind Your Own Business
Christobel Mattingley	Black Dog The Jetty Brave With Ben
Judy Blume	Tales of a Fourth Grade Nothing Superfudge
Pat Hutchins	Follow That Bus The House that Sailed Away
Beverley Cleary	Ramona Henny and the Paper Route
Theodore Taylor	The Cay
Joan Aitken	A Necklace of Raindrops The Kingdom Under the Sea

Sensational Story Stoppers!

Quotes or comments that have 'hooked' the reader can be displayed in the room as they are shared.

Example from a Year 5/6:

"However, that is still not the whole tale. Often enough the blind old man did not tell the end of his stories, and so it is with one. It is about the world, and so long as this world exists, the story goes on and on, and who knows how it will end?"

From *The Sea People* by Jorg Müller and Jorg Steiner.

Example from a Prep/1:

'*I'll hit you with my bommy-Knocker.*'

From *The Hungry Giant* (Story Box)

4 Top Ten

At the end of every month or so, the children can put their preferences together so that the 'Top Ten' books for the month can be selected.

See lots of other good ideas in *The Reading Bug and How to Catch It*. Jan Bailes (1980)

Other Evaluation Procedures

The procedures discussed below are well known and will not be described in detail here. However, references are provided for readers who might like to check on details of the procedures or on the reading behaviours, skills and attitudes that the procedures 'highlight' for evaluation purposes.

Participation in Shared Book Experience

Shared-book experience with small groups of children provides an ideal opportunity for evaluation. The teacher can concentrate on one child and note various aspects of his or her reading behaviour, or the teacher can concentrate on one aspect of reading behaviour (e.g. retention of high use words as part of sight vocabulary) and note how each child in the group performs in this respect.

Two useful references for the teacher are: Don Holdaway, *The Foundations of Literacy*, Ashton Scholastic, 1979 and the Teachers' Manuals for the 'Story Box' materials (Butler, 1984). Both outline the shared-book procedure but also help the teacher know what to look for.

Participation in Directed Reading-Thinking Activities

This procedure is outlined in Ann Pulvertaft's book, *Let's Breed Readers* (Ashton Scholastic, 1982). For a more detailed description, see 'Group instruction by directed reading-thinking activities'. chapter 6 in Russell Stauffer's book, *The Language-Experience Approach to the Teaching of Reading* (Harper & Row, 1970).

Directed Reading-Thinking Activities encourage children to predict, confirm or reject their predictions, and self-correct when necessary. As shown in chapter 9, these are very important comprehension strategies. A Directed Reading-Thinking Activity is therefore a very useful procedure for developing and monitoring comprehension strategies *while children are reading.* During the procedure, the teacher can evaluate one child's overall performance, or the use of a specific strategy by all children. *Many of the behaviours, understandings, skills and attitudes listed in the 'Reading Records' can be evaluated during a directed reading-thinking activity.*

The Primary Language program published by Heinemann includes an excellent set of cards specially produced for D.R.T.A.s.

Participation in Co-operative Cloze

Co-operative cloze, which is another small group procedure, also provides opportunities for the teacher to develop and monitor important reading strategies. This procedure is also outlined in Ann Pulvertaft's book, *Let's Breed Readers.*

Again, the teacher may choose to evaluate the performance of one child during the procedure, or to evaluate one aspect of reading behaviour across the whole group. The cloze passage can be prepared to focus the readers' attention on meaning (semantics), flow of language (syntax) or graphophonic features.

Small Group Procedures and Oral Language

These small group procedures also allow the teacher to evaluate each child's ability to work within a group. Co-operative talk, oral language skills and 'thinking aloud' all come to the surface. The teacher can evaluate many aspects of oral language. Joan Dalton, in *Adventures in Thinking* (Nelson, 1985, pp.7-8) provides a useful framework for observing use of oral language. The framework is based on the work of Joan Tough (1976, 1977) and the interested reader is referred to those texts.

Cloze Testing

Cloze techniques are best used as *teaching* procedures. They are most efficient in developing many reading strategies and skills and in helping children gain insights into the nature of reading. Each of the 'teaching' cloze procedures can be used to evaluate children's reading behaviours in 'natural' reading situations and we believe that this is the most valid and informative use of the various cloze procedures. We don't *need* separate–formal–assessment cloze procedures.

A formal cloze procedure that has been developed is outlined below. It is of some use in determining whether reading material is at frustration level, teaching level or independent level for a particular child. That is, it was developed primarily to assess whether or not materials were appropriate for individual children, not to assess the children themselves. This procedure requires a passage of at least 250-300 words. The first and last sentences are left intact, but the rest of the text has every fifth word deleted (except proper nouns). This cloze procedure accepts as correct only the *exact* word deleted. When these conditions apply (every fifth word deleted and exact replacements) then the following percentages are used to determine reading level:

Frustration level	Instruction level	Independent level
	40% 60%	

These scores are *approximate* indicators only and teachers still need to make judgements.

It has been found that this more formal use of cloze testing is appropriate only in upper primary grades and post-primary levels. In addition, such a cloze procedure cannot be used for assessing children unless the teachers look beyond the percentages and ask 'why' deletions were filled in as they were. The children must also be completely familiar with cloze procedures in general, for unless they have experience in completing cloze tasks and know what is required of them, a cloze test is totally inappropriate.

Since teachers can gain valuable information about silent reading strategies from all cloze procedures, it is even more unnecessary to be limited by the 'fifth word deletion' procedure for assessment. A particularly useful reference is 'Cloze Procedure Applications to Assessment of Silent Reading' (in Unsworth, ed., *Reading: An Australian Perspective*, Nelson, 1985).

Oral Reading Performance

A child's oral reading performance can tell the teacher much about the reading strategies being employed by the reader and provides valuable diagnostic information

The Goodmans and others, in the late 60s and during the 70s, studied children's oral reading behaviour and developed significant new ways of thinking about reading. Techniques were developed to harness the information provided through oral reading. The original *Reading Miscue Inventory* (Goodman and Burke, 1972) was too detailed and time consuming for classroom teachers. Since then Goodman, Watson and Burke have outlined new simplified procedures ('Reading Miscue Inventory', Richard Owen, 1986). Procedure 1 is the original procedure of 1972. Procedure 2, developed in 1976, looks at miscues at the sentence level, with several questions being asked of each miscue. Procedure 3 is the simplest. It looks at miscues at the sentence level within the context of the whole story and only three questions are asked about each miscue:

a is the sentence as produced by the child syntactically acceptable within the story?
b is the sentence as produced by the child semantically acceptable within the story?
c is there a meaning change within the story?

The miscues can be simply scored in the margin with a Y for "Yes" or an N for No (for Question 3 a P for "Partial" may be recorded). Procedures 2 and 3 provide simple ways of monitoring reading performance, of collecting information about miscues and evaluating the reader's use of cues and strategies.

Other attempts to shorten the procedure include the *B.R.I.M. or Brennan Record for the Interpretation of Miscues* (Brennan & Williams, 1978) and part of the *Reading Appraisal Guide* (Johnson, 1979).

Even the simplified instruments could involve the teacher in unnecessary analysis. Teachers only need to use them when they want more specific information about children who are having difficulty with reading or with children whose reading behaviours are unexplained.

Teachers who understand the principles involved in miscue analysis are very well equipped to listen to children read and to understand *why* they are reading that way. When teachers have such information, they are in a good position to help the reader with positive strategies for reading.

Clay (1979) has recommended the use of 'running records' to evaluate children's oral reading performance and to thereby gain information about their reading strategies. 'Running records' are also records of the miscues children make while reading orally from the material which is being used for instruction. Clay suggests shorthand ways of recording these miscues and provides information on how to interpret them.

Recognition of Personal Words

Teachers often wish to test recognition of words, especially at the beginning stage of reading. If this is so, then it is much more appropriate to test words which come from the child's **personal word bank** or **personal dictionary.** These words would have been used by the child, in meaningful contexts, before becoming part of the word bank or dictionary.

Word Recognition tests, with lists of unrelated words or words which the child has not chosen to use, require the child to use only graphophonic information. This 'minimal reading situation' does *not* reflect the child's real reading ability, when words are in context. Direct recall or memory is tested in this way, not *reading.*

Pupil Self-Evaluation

An important aim of primary education is to help children become independent learners. This cannot happen if the teacher's role is always one of prescribing exactly what the children will do, how they will do it and when they will do it. If we expect children to think for themselves and take some responsibility for their learning, they must be given opportunities to make some decisions themselves.

An individualized reading program includes self-selection of books, self-pacing and a self-evaluation component. The belief that self-selection of books is important does not mean that the teacher never prescribes some reading materials; the belief that self-pacing must be developed does not mean that the teacher has no expectations of each child. Obviously too, the belief that children should be able to evaluate their own work does not mean that the teacher is not involved in evaluation. **Both teacher and child are important partners in promoting learning.**

Nicoll (1980) reminds us that self-evaluation cannot be imposed suddenly; it must develop slowly. This development is assisted by:

1 Developing an environment for self-evaluation in which the teacher's evaluation is positive and helps children know what they know.
2 Promoting individual achievement rather than competitive assessment. ('Honest self-criticism is unlikely to occur if the goal is to be better than everybody else.')
3 Evaluating in specific terms that highlight specific strengths or indicate problems *and their solutions*. (Vague terms such as 'satisfactory' and 'could do better' give children no advice about what might be done.)
4 Involving children in daily decisions about evaluation and encouraging them to keep some of their own records.
(Nicoll, 1980, pp.204-5)

Self-evaluation should be part of the daily program, regardless of the curriculum area. Self-evaluation helps children to think about what they are doing and what they need to do. It helps them to know what they are learning and enables the teacher to emphasize self-improvement rather than comparison with someone else. (Comparisons are useful for *program* evaluation but do little for helping one's own achievement.)

A student self-evaluation form, which can be amended to suit personal concerns, is included in Appendix 1. However, *children will need assistance* when they are first required to make entries on such a form. The purpose of the form should be discussed with them and adequate time must be allowed to complete the relevant section. (The form will be completed over many months; it will never be completed in one sitting!)

References

Bailes, J. (ed), *The Reading Bug and How to Catch it*, Ashton Scholastic, 1980.

Brennan, M. & Williams, P., *The Brennan Record for the Interpretation of Miscues*, Literacy Centre, Riverina College, Wagga Wagga, NSW, 1978.

Butler, A., *The Story Box in the Classroom — Stage 1*, Rigby, 1984.

——, *The Story Box in the Classroom — Stages 2-7*, Rigby, 1984.

Cambourne, B., 'Assessing Comprehension Strategies Using Class Texts' in Unsworth, L. (ed), *Reading: an Australian Perspective*, Nelson, 1985.

——, 'Assessment in Reading': The Drunkard's Search' in Unsworth, L. (ed), *Reading: An Australian Perspective*, Nelson, 1985.

Clay, M., *The Early Detection of Reading Difficulties: A Diagnostic Survey with Recovery Procedures*, Heinemann Educational Books, 1979.

Dalton, J., *Adventures in Thinking*, Nelson, 1985.

Education Department of Victoria, *Ministerial Paper 6: Curriculum Development and Planning in Victoria*, 1984.

——, *Submission to 'Basic Learning in Primary Schools', program*, 1985.

Gilmour H. & Tyrer, D., *Reading On*, Education Department of Victoria, 1985.

Goodman, Y. & Burke, C., *Reading Strategies: Focus on Comprehension*, Holt, Rinehart and Winston, 1980.

——, *Reading Miscue Inventory,* 1972.

Holdaway, D., *The Foundations of Literacy*, Ashton Scholastic, 1979.

Johnson, B., *Reading Appraisal Guide*, Australian Council for Educational Research, 1979.

Kemp, M., *Watching Children Read & Write*, Nelson, 1987.

Kemp, M., 'Standardized Tests and Reading-for-not-Reading' in Unsworth, L. (ed), *Reading: An Australian Perspective*, Nelson, 1985.

MacGinitie, W. 1973 'What Are We Testing?' in Walter H. MacGinitie, (ed), *Assessment Problems in Reading*, Newark, Del., International Reading Association, pp.35-43.

Nicoll, V., 'How Can Pupil Self-Evaluation be Developed?' in *101 Questions Primary Teachers Ask*, Primary English Teaching Association, 1980.

Pulvertaft, A., *Let's Breed Readers*, Ashton Scholastic, 1982.

Pyrczak, F. 1972, 'Objective Evaluation of the Quality of Multiple Choice Test Items Designed to Measure Comprehension of Reading Passages', *Reading Research Quarterly*, 8: 62-71.

Stauffer, R., *The Language Experience Approach to the Teaching of Reading*, Harper & Row, 1970.

Strang, R. 1968, *Reading Diagnosis and Remediation*, Newark, Del.; International Reading Association.

Tough, J., *Listening to Children Talking*, Ward Lock Educational, 1976.

——, *Talking and Learning*, Ward Lock Educational, 1977.

Tuinman, J. 1973 'Determining the Passage Dependency of Comprehension Questions in Five Major Tests'. *Reading Research Quarterly*, 9: 206-23.

Unsworth, L., 'Cloze Procedure Applications to Assessment of Silent Reading' in Unsworth, L. (ed), *Reading: An Australian Perspective*, Nelson, 1985.

——, (ed), *Reading: An Australian Persective*, Nelson, 1985.

Vaughan, J., 'Evaluation' in Walshe, R., (ed), *101 Questions Primary Teachers Ask*, Primary English Teaching Association, 1980.

Weaver, W & Bickley, A., 1967, 'Sources of Information for Responses to Reading Test Items'. Proceedings 75th Annual Convention, American Psychological Association, pp. 293-92.

Winkley, C. 1971, 'What Do Diagnostic Tests Really Diagnose?' in R. Leibert, (ed), *Diagnostic Viewpoints in Reading*, Newark, Del., International Reading Association, pp.64-80.

13 Reading Classrooms in Action

Teachers Accounts of their Reading Classrooms

The following accounts of 'Reading Class-rooms in Action' were written by teachers in the Northern Metropolitan Region of the Education Department of Victoria.

Each of the teachers had developed individualized, literature-based approaches to reading and small group conferences were a feature of their programs. The librarian helped teachers with the planning of introductory activities and also used many features of the program during library sessions with the children.

The contributors:

Jill Holmes   Prep to Year 3
                 Yan Yean Primary School

Sue Sparkes   Year 1
                 Yallambie Primary School

Russell Feben   Year 5
                 Mill Park Primary School

Kay Sagar   Librarian
                 Mill Park Primary School

Jill's Classroom

Prep to Year 3
Teaching and learning are interdependent. The longer I teach, the more I learn.

Working in a small rural school, I learnt that children make demands on each other that I never would have considered, let alone put into practice. It was common for children of either sex from the upper school to urge the infants to hurry with their lunches. They were needed to make up the numbers for the lunch-time cricket or rounders game.

Similarly, the older children voluntarily joined in morning talk, sang nursery rhymes and played in the sand pit. Once again, I never would have considered asking them to.

Following the unorthodox example, I read class serials which I would never have considered suitable for an infant room. The preps laughed out loud at the machinations of the Bottersnikes and Gumbles, and revelled in Roald Dahl's more unsavoury characters. They also worked their way through at least one volume of Joan Aitken's stories. Needless to say, the older children, when given the choice, enjoyed picture story books and fairy tales.

I had always had a daily silent reading period when teaching middle and upper grades. Since everything else was not going according to plan, why not include the infants in this time?

Accordingly, for an initial period of ten minutes each day, the preps armed themselves with books, magazines or journals and sat quietly in the reading corner. As time went by, the silent reading period was increased to twenty minutes. There were two reasons for this. One was to give the older children a longer time to enjoy their reading without distraction. The second was simply to extend the time that the infants found pleasurable.

Their choice of silent reading material varied greatly. They were usually keen to read whatever I had read aloud to the class, so I was careful to balance serial reading with picture story books, poems and rhymes.

Class and individually made books were also very popular. These were borrowed regularly for home consumption as well as during silent reading periods. Books made in school were the first books which were taken home to be shared with parents.

Subsequent material to be taken home was chosen by the children, in consultation with myself. Commercially prepared nursery rhymes were very popular. The children responded to the predictability and rhythm, as well as enjoying the illustrations and familiarity of these books.

Although the school did not possess a 'reading scheme' which extended into the infant areas, the children did come to know what a 'reader' is. They learnt that a reader is not something to be taken home at night, recited to an anxious parent and ticked off on a list next day. They learnt that a reader is a person who sits down quietly and reads with pleasure a book of one's own choice. Once, I would not have considered asking it of them. The longer I teach, the more I learn.

Jill Holmes
P-3
Yan Yean Primary School

Sue's Classroom

Year 1
At the school, published reading schemes are used as one strand of the school program. However, two other strands are equally important. One is an experience-based approach (language experience) which incorporates the reading done through the writing program, and the other very important strand is children's literature.

At the start of the year, the main emphasis was on published reading scheme material. I found that many of the children progressed 'through the levels' satisfactorily but that several did not. However, *none* of the children had that zest for reading which was one of my main aims. Consequently, I began to rely less on the published schemes and began to introduce more children's literature, song charts, poetry charts, joke books, wall stories, and so on. (One of the published schemes, the new edition of Young Australia, actually helped me to do this, as the Teacher's Manual was full of ideas and activities.) With the wider variety of material I had introduced into the room, USSR time suddenly changed. The children knew that immediately after USSR time, they would have the opportunity to participate in follow-up activities related to their reading. At first, USSR time lasted for only 5 or 6 minutes. By June, I would allow 20 minutes for silent reading (far beyond my expectations!) before announcing that the children could chat with a friend about their books. However, many of the children would choose to continue reading silently for another 5 or 10 minutes. They simply didn't want to stop!

I had found what it was that I had to provide to get that 'zest' I was looking for. The children's enthusiasm astounded me.

One of my initial concerns was how an emphasis on the literature strand would affect the 'slow achievers'. Leigh, a boy who had struggled through some of the early 'readers' of the schemes, discovered *A Fly Went By* (Mike McClintock) and 'took off'. The humour, combined with the rhyme and rhythm of the text, were ingredients which worked for him. When he then tackled *One Fish Two Fish, Red Fish Blue Fish* and had success with that too, he was so proud, that he read pages alternately with other children and shared his enthusiasm with the rest of the class.

When Leigh was trying to cope with the controlled vocabulary and promotion through levels, he saw himself as a failure and acted accordingly. When he had initial success with humorous books full of interesting language, reading took on a whole new dimension for him. Leigh finally experienced personal success and satisfaction with reading. He knew it and everyone else knew it! His success caused a chain reaction and he began to approach other curriculum areas with more confidence and enthusiasm too.

I *knew* that the children were making progress (many of them were achieving much more than I had hoped for). At the end of the year, when A.C.E.R. reading tests were administered by the school, *all* of the children scored stanines of 6 or above! Most of them scored 7, 8 or 9. Not one child scored 5 (average) or below. The standardized test results confirmed that the children had made excellent progress, but their keen desire to read and to share was my major reward.

Sue Sparkes (McFarlane)
Year 1
Yallambie Primary School

Russell's Classroom

Year 5

At the start of the year our main source of reading material was the school reading scheme (mainly the new edition of Young Australia), the school library and what the children brought from home.

The other Year 5 teacher and I collected a wide variety of literature and recorded titles on whole class charts so it was available for children to borrow. The published material was used mainly for small teaching groups.

The first few weeks of term were spent establishing routines with children. I emphasized that what they decided to read during silent reading time would be their choice. If they found a book that did not meet their needs then they were free to return it and select again. I wanted them to become responsible for their reading and to understand that I would value their choices.

Initially, I found that children often chose unwisely. Some chose easier books so that they would 'whip' through them quickly; others would choose books far too difficult and would have to select again. To me, this was all part of the process of coming to terms with what they wanted from their reading. I stressed again and again that I wanted them to enjoy their reading and if they weren't happy with a book then they were to get rid of it or talk with me.

By second term, unwise choices were rarely a problem. The children thought it was great and their confidence grew as they learned more about different authors and styles of writing. They knew what they were looking for and what they wanted to get out of their reading material. Peer recommendations played a major role as we discussed and shared books together.

Initially, my reading program was kept very structured, as I needed to be able to keep tabs on 30 children reading, in total, perhaps 12 to 15 different titles! Question sheets to cover fiction and non-fiction titles were organized and the children were expected to use these as a guide when they finished a book. As the year progressed, both these sheets and my requirements become more flexible but also more demanding. Even if the children found a book uninteresting, they were expected to record in their reading book *why* they did not wish to continue with it.

Having read a book and written a comment, they would sometimes complete an activity of their choice related to the reading. Some great models, posters, advertisements and so on resulted from this.

Short, individual conferences were a very

important part of the program. After reading a book, children would put their names on the conference board. Each child would share something about the book with me. At first, I had to guide them and do most of the talking, but they learned very quickly to discuss books with me and I was surprised by their ability to do so. I was also very pleased when the previously reluctant readers got involved and pressured me for conferences. A short record was kept of each conference and proved valuable as part of my overall evaluation.

As a result of children reading the same title or works by the same author, we started having group conferences. These were most valuable, as the children also learned from each other.

Books from the 'Young Australia' reading scheme still played a significant part in group work directed by me. However, I used titles, or selections within titles, selectively. Many of the selections were great for cloze activities or Directed Reading—Thinking Activities. Many also provided an excellent stimulus for further reading of literature books, and others tied in very closely with parts of the social studies and science programs.

I found it difficult at first to get things set up and routines established. At times, it seemed chaotic and I'd think how much easier it would be (for me!) if I just *told* the children what to read all the time. But then it all began to come together and by the end of term one, the kids loved the reading session each day. They became independent in many ways and this further freed me to spend time with individual children.

The children's attitudes to reading improved tremendously and it was nice to be in the position of the children recommending books to me rather than the other way around. I learned a lot more about authors and the world of literature myself. In retrospect, I can look back over the year and see it as a year's in-service education for me!

Russell Feben
Year 5
Mill Park Primary School

Kay — Librarian

I have been librarian at this school for four years, during which time I have seen dramatic changes in several areas.

My first recollection of the early days in the library was that children were unable to borrow books. There were several reasons for this of course. Mill Park was a new school with limited library resources and the children had had little or no library experience (there is no municipal library in the area either). However, the major reason was that they had no background in literature; they had not developed an awareness of what books have to offer. Their reading experience was very narrow and they had had little exposure to different forms of literature.

I found that all the children had to go through a stage of reading the sort of literature which is sometimes referred to as 'fodder'. Even the Year 6 children would read 'Paddington Bear' stories, 'My Naughty Little Sister' stories, 'Encyclopedia Brown' stories, and so on. However, the reading of this 'fodder' seems to be a necessary stage that most if not all children go through. (For example, most good readers I know have all devoured Enid Blyton books in their earlier years!) This type of literature has simple language structures, no difficult vocabulary, and simple plots that the children can easily follow. It helps to get them into the reading habit and to develop their self-confidence. However, children in the upper school were still stuck on this 'fodder'.

After the introduction of literature-based programs in several of the classrooms, the children's interest in books and reading exploded! Within months, children's attitudes and interests were changing in ways I could not have anticipated. Now, I find children asking for books written by specific authors such as Susan Cooper, J.R.R. Tolkien, Ivan Southall, Ruth Park . . . authors they'd never heard of before!

In my first year at the school, I can remember saying to the Year 6 children that I would like each of them to try reading, say, *The Phantom Tollbooth* by the end of the year. Their reaction was one of disinterest. Now, I find that I'm swamped with requests not only for the books

I suggest, but for many other titles as well. I continually find that I need to do something about the supply of literature available to the children. After the first explosion of interest in reading, it was necessary for me to put in a submission for extra funding.

One thing I have found particularly exciting. When children ask me for help in selecting a book, I generally suggest several titles with a short description about each one. Children have often said, 'But I tried that last year and it was too hard' or 'I just wasn't interested in that one.' I remind them that that *was* last year and that they have read many books since then. They are usually prepared to give it a go. The exciting thing is that they often come back to me and tell me in a great rush, 'But it was great!'

I have noticed too that many of the teachers are now using the library as the 'reading scheme'. This seems more than sensible to me, considering the amount of money spent in the library and the 'real books' they can find there. Libraries and reading programs should never be separate.

Personally, I have also found that working *with* classroom teachers has many advantages. The library session becomes a part of the children's total reading program and the classroom teacher and I are backing each other up and providing a much richer and more varied program. I'm happier because I feel a 'part' of the school, and in turn, I can provide more relevant asistance.

But mostly, I'm happier because I have most children reading a wider variety of materials, borrowing more regularly, discussing books and authors with me and reading at levels well beyond the 'fodder' that used to be consumed by only the few rare bookworms.

In *17* years of teaching, I've not seen such a dramatic change in reading habits, enjoyment of books and knowledge of titles and authors.

Kay Sagar
Mill Park Primary School

Some Children's Comments

I love share time because its grouse to share your book. When I am in share time I am very confident.

Amber

Share Time gets me into thicker books and different books because people recommend them to me.

Christine

Share times are good because they get people interested in the books you've read and you can have a conference together when you've all read them. I like starting things.

Dean

I think I like reading heaps more now because I'm finding books that I like by myself.

Glenn

I like the reading program because the teachers don't tell you what you have to read and you can pick your own reading books.

Trudi

I like the reading program because you can pick your own book. I think I'm going good because I've read lots of books I like. I reckon that's good for me.

Matthew

Last year I used to read a book just because of its title or its look. Now I know how to pick a book — sometimes it takes a while.

Tabitha

Sometimes I read a book and I really like it and wish it would never end. Other times I try to hurry and finish it because I want to find out what happens!

Tanya

14 A WIZARD OF EARTHSEA

A Wizard of Earthsea, by Ursula Le Guin, tells the exciting adventures of Ged as he travels the islands of the Earthsea archipelago. It is a story about the struggle between good and evil. Ged's pride caused the loosing of the Shadow Beast, which then haunted his life in many different ways. It did not stop following Ged until he had the courage to turn and 'hunt the hunter'. He finally faced the shadow after he had pursued it to the very edge of the archipelago.

A Wizard of Earthsea is a popular fantasy enjoyed by many readers, but often left until the post-primary years. However, upper primary school children also enjoy the book immensely. Capable readers have chosen to read the book independently, but with teacher involvement, the book is excellent for a literature group. Consequently, the procedure outlined below is not typical, but it is an alternative procedure which can help children tackle literature that they might not tackle on their own. The teacher's role was to be a member of the literature group and to read the novel at the same time as the children. In this way, the teacher and children could meet regularly for conferences. This enabled the teacher to monitor the children's understanding of the book as they read and also enabled the children to seek clarification while they were reading. This was necessary to help the children adapt to the style of language and become familiar with the unusual vocabulary.

Six children from Year 5, who had shown a particular interest in fantasy, came together as a group to read *A Wizard of Earthsea*. Before reading started, the teacher prepared the children by:

- distributing books and promoting discussion about the title, the front cover illustration and the map of Earthsea;
- distributing copies of a blank map of Earthsea;
- distributing blank sheets with chapter headings;
- talking about the characteristics of fantasy.

The blank maps were to be used while the children were reading the book so that they could show the most important islands and the journey that Ged took. The sheets with the chapter headings were for jotting down characters' names, main points and places the children wanted to note.

Each day, the children were to read a chapter during the Silent Reading part of the session and at home if necessary. After the first chapter was read, the group met together with the teacher. They had written down, under the chapter heading ('Warriors in the Mist') what they thought was the most important information. This included the names of characters introduced. They also located the island of Gont and marked it on their maps. (Samples of some of the children's work along the way are shown below.) They then determined when they would meet to discuss chapter 2.

After each chapter, they continued writing down independently what they thought were the main points. When they met together, they then had to compare their points and justify or modify them if necessary. This proved to be a particularly valuable activity and was excellent for starting discussion during the conference. The children often referred to the text and read passages orally to support their opinions or to check on their understanding. After chapter 3, the children themselves decided to make a chart to keep recording places, people and things.

This chart proved to be a very helpful guide to continued reading.

The teacher had intended to continue chapter by chapter for some time, but after the fourth chapter, the children had come to terms with the author's style of writing, the characters and the storyline and just had to read on!

However, the children had enjoyed the conferences and demanded that they continue at regular intervals. This allowed them to compare their 'main points' sheets and maps and to discuss the 'Places, People and Things' chart as well as anything of interest or concern to them.

After the book was finished, the children worked in pairs to finish three activity sheets (one on the islands and the characters and events there; one on 'the power' and one on 'the shadow'). They also completed a cloze activity based on the book. The children certainly did not need these activities to help them understand the book, but they enjoyed the book and the 'togetherness' so much that they wanted to continue with activities after the actual reading was finished.

Samples of the Children's Work

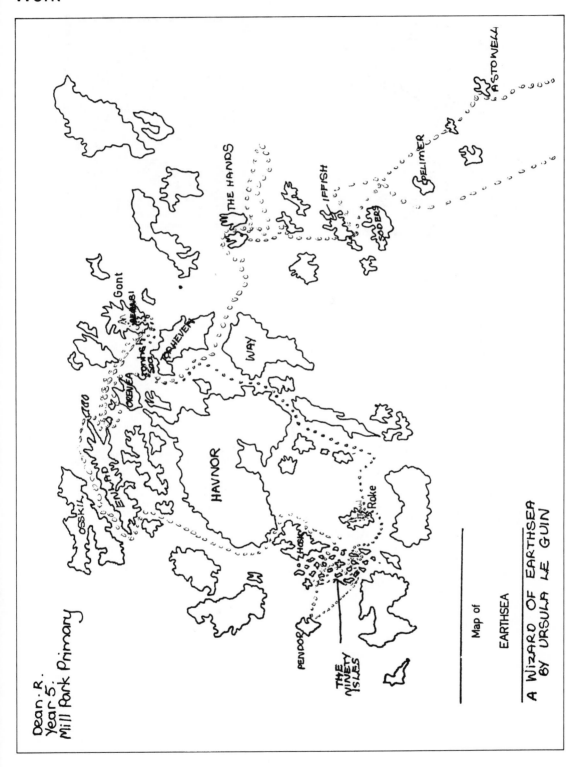

Dean. R.
Year 5.
Mill Park Primary

Map of

EARTHSEA

A WIZARD OF EARTHSEA
BY URSULA LE GUIN

Brenton Hall
Year 5
Mill Park

1 *Warriors in the Mist*

① Geds first name he had
was Duny.
② On his thirteenth birthday Duny
was named Ged
③ Geds Aunt was a witch and tau
-ght him some spells.

④ Ged saved Gont from the Kargs
by using a spell.
⑤ The spell made fog so the Kargs
could not see.

⑥ Ged went as pratice with
a mage who had given him
a name
Sparrow haw Duny
— Ged, mage, Father, Aunt,
Brothers

2 *The Shadow*

① Ged thought he would
be taught tricks quickly
② Ged gets angry when
he is not taught many
tricks.
③ Ogion, who is Ged's master
asked him to go to Roke.
Ged went
④ Unleased shadow

Dean·R.

1 Warriors in the Mist

GED LIVED IN GONT
HIS MOTHERS SISTER IS A WITCH
HIS FARTHER IS A FORGER
HE HAS SIX OLDER BROTHERS
HE HAS THE POWERS OF A WIZARD
HE HAS BEEN TAKEN AS AN APPRENTICE BY THE
MAGE OF RE ALBI

DUNY-GED (MOTHER) FARTHER AUNT-WITCH
SIX BROTHERS MAGE OF RE-ALBI

2 The Shadow

THE MAGE WOULD NOT SHOW HIM ANY MAGIC
THEY HEADED TOWARDS RE ALBI WITH
THE HARDSHIPS OF ADVENTURE
THE LORD OF RE ALBIS WIFE IS AN
ENCHANTRESS
HER DAUTER IS ALREADY WITCH LIKE
GED CAN SUMMON THE DEAD
HE IS NOT GOOD AT SEA BUT HAS GOOD
EYE SIGHT

MAGE OF RE-ALBI GED ENCHANTRESS
DAUGHTER SHIP MATES SHIP MASTER

Dean. R.

9 Iffish

GED LEFT THE WEST HAND IN HIS NEW
BOAT LOOKFAR HE WENT TO ANOTHER
ISLAND IN WHICH HE LEFT SOON BECAUSE
THE PEOPLE HAD SEEN STRANGE SIGHTINGS
OF HIM HE DID NOT KNOW ABOUT.

GED WENT TO IFFISH AND THE SAME
SIGHTINGS HAD BEEN SEEN, ON IFFISH
HE MET HIS OLD FRIEND VETCH WHO
DECIDED TO JOIN HIM IN THE HUNT
AND THE NEXT MORNING THEY
SET OF INTO THE OPEN SEA.

10 The Open Sea

ON THIER HUNT FOR THE SHADOW
THEY STOPPED ON THE LAST LAND
ON WHICH THEY WERE TOLD THERE
WERE NO MORE LANDS FROM THERE

THEY MET THE SHADOW ON A
SAND COVERED SEA GED SAID ITS
NAME AND IT DISAPPERED FROM
THE FACE OF THE EARTH

THEY SAILED BACK TO IFFISH
AND WERE GREATED WARMLY
BY MUREE AND YARROW

THE END

Brenton

9 Iffish

① Ged went to a place called Vemish. He was told someone who cast no shadow, had passed by.

② A man gave Ged a boat and Ged sailed to Iffish.

③ He met Vetch, and they talked about what had happened to Ged. Vetch went with Ged to seek the shadow

10 The Open Sea

① They sailed to Soders and onto Astowell.

② The people there said there was no land beyond.

③ They sailed and saw the shadow on an Island. Ged said to the shadow "Ged". That was its name.

④ THE SHADOW WAS

DEFEATED

Sasha

Shadow Beast!

APPENDIX 1

Reproducible Sheets

a) 'Thinking about my Reading' — Informational Books   (Level I)
b) 'Thinking about my Reading' — Fiction books   (Level I)
c) 'Thinking about my Reading' — Fiction books   (Level II)
d) 'Thinking about my Reading' — Informational Books   (Level II)
e) Interest Inventory
f) 'Books I've Read'
g) Individual Conference Log
h) Reading Record — Beginning Readers
i) Reading Record — Developing Readers
j) Stages of Development in a First Year Program
k) 'Am I developing as an Independent Reader?'
   (student self-evaluation form)

The following pages can be used to develop reproducible pages. Teachers should feel free to adapt and illustrate them to suit their particular needs.

'Thinking about my Reading'

These sheets are provided at two different levels. Level I sheets may be appropriate for the middle primary years but should also be used with upper primary children who have not participated before in an individualized, literature-based program.

Remember: these sheets contain guiding questions only. They may help children to think about and respond to their reading. Teachers should use them to help the children discover and articulate the questions *they* want to ask.

Reading Records

The reading records provide for detailed evaluation of children's reading. However, some teachers of children in their first year at school may also wish to use the sheets, 'Stages of Development in a First Year Program' (adapted from Holdaway; 1979, 1980). The sheets will often be used into and during a child's second year at school as well.

Thinking about my Reading

Informational Books   *Level I*

1 What is the book about?
2 Who is the author?
3 When was your book published?
4 Was the book easy to read? Why? Why not?
5 Did the book have pictures, charts, maps, graphs, tables or photos?
6 Did these help you to understand the information better?
7 What were some 'topic' words the author used?
8 What was your favourite part?
9 Did the author tell you enough? What else would you like to know?
10 What did you find out that you didn't know before?
11 What other books are there on this topic? (Check in the library.)
12 Share what you have found out with a friend.

Thinking about my Reading

Fiction Books   *Level I*

Author
1 What do you know about the author?
2 What is the author trying to tell you in your book?
3 What did the author have to know about to write this book?
4 What sorts of things does your author like or dislike? (people, places, behaviour, feelings)

Characters (people, animals, toys . . .)
1 Who are the main characters in your story?
2 Do you like them? Tell me why.
3 Do you dislike them? Tell me why.
4 Choose one character. Why is this character important in the story?
5 Do you know anyone like the characters?
6 Do any of the characters change?
7 Do any characters do things that you think are good?
8 Do any characters do things that you think are wrong?

The Story
Plot
1 Tell me the main things that happened in your story.
2 Were you able to guess what was going to happen at the end?
3 Can you think of another way your story might have ended?
4 What do you think was the best part of the story? Why?

Setting
1 Where does the story take place?
2 Tell me what the place was like.
3 Have you ever been to a place like this?
4 Did the story take place a long time ago?
5 Is it about the future?
6 Is it happening now?

Mood
1 How did you feel while reading the book?
2 Why did you feel that way?
3 What was the funniest part?
4 What was the saddest part?
5 What was the most exciting thing that happened or the strangest thing that happened?
6 What do you remember most about the story?

Style
1 What special words does the author use to help you?
   ● hear things in the story?
   ● see things in the story?
2 Tell me about any pictures the author has left in your mind.
3 What do you like about the way the author has written the story?

Thinking about my Reading

Fiction Books   *Level II*

Author

1 What do you know about the author?
2 Why do you think the author wrote the book?
3 What is the author trying to tell us?
4 What do we learn about the personality or the interests of the author?
5 What did the author have to know to write the book?

Characters

(The questions below assume that the main characters are people, but they are relevant even when the main characters are animals, toys or whatever.)

1 Who are the main characters?
2 What kind of people are they?
3 Do you like/dislike them? Why?
4 Why are they important in the story?
5 Why did they behave as they did?
6 Do you know anyone like them?
7 How do they change throughout the story?
8 How are the characters different/alike?
9 Are people really like these characters?
10 Was the behaviour of a particular character right or wrong?

The Story
Plot:
1 What happened in the story? What was the sequence of events?
2 What might have happened if a certain action had not taken place?
3 Were you able to predict the ending?
4 What other way might the story have ended?
5 Under a heading (such as People, Animals, Places, Things) list important words.
6 Which chapter do you think is the most important to the story? Why?

Setting:
1 Where did the story take place?
2 What was the place like?
3 Could there be a place like this? Do you know of a place like this?
4 When did the story take place? (past, present, future)
5 Which part of the story best describes the setting?
6 How does the writer create the atmosphere for the setting?
7 Are there any particular words that create this atmosphere?

Mood:
1 How did you feel while reading the book? Why did you feel that way?
2 What was the saddest/funniest incident?
3 What was the most exciting/unusual/mysterious incident?
4 How did the author make you feel the way you did?
5 What do you remember most about the story?
6 Does the mood of the story change? How?

Style:
1 How did the author describe the characters?
2 Were there any unusual ways of saying things?
3 Does the author give you enough information?
4 How does the author keep you interested?
5 What special words does the author use to help you hear, see, smell, taste or feel things?
6 What pictures has the author's writing left in your mind?
7 What strengths does the author have? What do you like about his/her style?

Thinking about my Reading

Informational Books   *Level II*

Content:
1 What is the book about?
2 Was the information presented clearly?
3 Did the title mislead you? (Did you expect to discover information that wasn't there?)
4 Did the content of the book give you enough information? If not, what else do you need to know? Will you need to go to other books?

Accuracy:
1 Who is the author? Is the author well qualified to write about this topic? (Check book jacket; title page; introduction; foreword; other books.)
2 Does the book provide up-to-date information? (Check publishing date. Are there any revised editions? Are there more recent books about the same topic?)
3 Does the author let you know when he/she is stating a fact or expressing an opinion? (Look for key words such as 'I think . . .' or 'Scientists believe . . .' or 'As far as we know . . .' or 'Perhaps . . .')

Style
1 Is the author's style clear and direct?
2 Was information well organized?
3 Is the information told straight to you or is it given in story form?
4 Does the book make you want to learn more about your topic?

Illustrations:
1 Were illustrations used?
2 Did the author use diagrams, photographs, maps, charts, graphs, tables?
3 If so, did these help you to understand the text better? If labels and captions were used, did they help?

Organization:
1 Did you use the Table of Contents or the Index?
2 Did they help you to find information quickly?
3 Did headings and sub-headings help you to 'see' what was in the book?

Interest Inventory
_____

Name:_____Date_____

My family

Our pets

My hobbies

Places I have lived in or visited

Important things that have happened to me

What I usually do after school/during the weekend

Favourite TV program(s)

Favourite book(s)

Books I have enjoyed

Favourite author(s)

Authors I know

Illustrators I know

Things I would like to read about

Name:

Books I've Read		
Title/Author	Date started	Date finished

Individual Conference Log

Name:

Date	Title/Author	Comments

Reading Record

		Name:_____		
		Year level:_____19_____		
Beginning Readers		Teacher:_____		

	Rarely	*Sometimes*	*Usually*	*Comments*
• **Attitude**				
able to enjoy books				
reads at other times				
shares with others				
borrows books freely				
maintains silent reading for an increasing length of time				
• **Concepts about Print**				
understands that print contains the message				
understands directional conventions				
understands concept of 'word'				
understands concept of 'letter'				
understands terminology: first, last, space, line, top, bottom, sentence				
knows meaning of . and ?				
demonstrates concepts about print in own writing				
• **Use of Textual Cues**				
uses context cues				
– semantic cues				
– syntactic cues				
– pictorial cues				
uses graphophonic cues				

	Rarely	Sometimes	Usually	Comments
● Reading Strategies & Comprehension expects the text to make sense more concerned to identify meaning than words or letters prepared to make predictions self-corrects when predictions are unsatisfactory processes chunks of language (doesn't read word by word)				
When in difficulty: reads on to end of sentence starts sentence again and re-reads uses initial letter as a cue and then guesses uses picture as a cue and then guesses				
After reading: can re-tell story in own words talks about characters recalls any main ideas recalls details understands developing sequence can describe setting knows whether s/he likes story and why				

	Rarely	Sometimes	Usually	Comments
● Shared Book Experience				
involved with text; shows obvious responses (laughs, frowns)				
asks for story to be read again				
comments about story				
asks questions about story				
joins in during subsequent readings				
makes comments or asks questions about print				
makes comments or asks questions about pictures				
retains 'high use' words as part of sight vocabulary				
selects story to be read independently				
● Selection				
generally selects appropriately				
selects different reading materials for different purposes				
asks someone else about book				

Reading Record

Developing Readers	Name: _____ Year level: _____ 19_____ Teacher: _____			
	Rarely	*Sometimes*	*Usually*	*Comments*
● Attitude *enjoys books; borrows freely* *reads at other times* *shares with others* *takes initiative* *reads silently for a sustained period*				
● Use of Textual Cues *uses context cues* *– semantic cues* *– syntactic cues* *– pictorial cues* *uses graphophonic cues*				
● Selection Skills *selects a variety of books independently* *seeks advice when necessary* *selects books appropriate to purpose* *uses library effectively*				

	Rarely	Sometimes	Usually	Comments
● Reading Strategies & Comprehension				
concerned with reading for meaning				
prepared to make predictions				
rejects unsatisfactory predictions and self-corrects				
does not make unnecessary self-corrections				
processes chunks of language (doesn't read word by word)				
can locate specific parts of text				
When in difficulty:				
reads on to end of sentence				
starts sentence again and re-reads				
uses initial letters or letter clusters as a cue and then predicts				
uses pictorial cues (including charts, graphs, etc.)				
After reading:				
can re-tell story or information in own words				
can discuss character development				
can recognize or infer main ideas details				
can recognize or infer sequence cause and effect comparisons				
can make judgements of reality and fantasy fact and opinion values				

	Rarely	Sometimes	Usually	Comments
● Oral Reading				
reads effectively with teacher				
prepares beforehand				
reads specific text to support a position taken				
considers audience				
gives attention to volume, pitch, intonation, expression, pace, breathing				
● Written Work				
uses 'guiding questions' when necessary				
writes own comments without reference to 'guiding questions'				
gives thoughtful consideration to written work				
comments or answers in sufficient detail				
writes legibly when necessary (considers reader)				
● Reference Materials				
uses reference books appropriately				
uses various non-book resources				
can find specific information				
can cope with demands of 'textbooks'				
presents effectively information acquired				

Stages of Development in a First-year Program

(Adapted from Holdaway, 1979, 1980)   Name:_____

Children will develop in different ways, but a progression of stages may be something like the following:

Stage 1   Emergent Reading

Processes favourite stories in reading-like ways approximating to book language.
No sequential text attention, but self-corrects for sense.
'Reads' back short experience stories written by the teacher.
Engages in writing-like scribble or invented symbols.
Attempts to copy or write over the teacher's script.
Comments:

Stage 2   Advanced Emergent Reading

Can follow a line of print in an enlarged text using word spaces.
Confirms and self-corrects by syntactic and semantic fit, and by word fit (i.e., knows there are too many or too few words).
Realizes that texts have the same reading every day — that print is a stable, word-by-word record of language.
Can find any word in a very familiar text by checking off from the beginning of a sentence — what we call 'matching'. Can locate the same word on a page of print.
Shows word spaces in writing-like behaviour.
Comments:

Stage 3   Emergent to Early Reading

Knows some words from day to day in context.
Predicts actively in new material using syntax and meaning.
Has developed stable directional habits in processing familiar print.
Can identify and name most letters.
Can visually recognize words that begin with the same letter.
Forms some letters in an identifiable way in copying and in writing.
Comments:

Stage 4   Early Reading

Knows the meaning of 'beginning' and 'end' as applied to word limits.
Can use some initial letter-sound associations to predict and confirm.
Can recognize the most common affixes (-ed, -ing, -s) when used with familiar root words.
Can manipulate known word-cards or sentence-parts into a sentence-sequence.
Knows the meaning of capitalization at the beginning of sentences and of full stops at the end, and sometimes uses these conventions in writing.
Comments:

Stage 5   Advanced Early Reading

In word-solving, uses many initial-consonant and some consonant-blend letter-sound relationships, together with context clues.
Can recognize letters associated with a sound heard in words, and can locate these for confirmation in the terminal and medial positions.
Probably displays 'voice-pointing', checking off each word in reading by some form of confirmatory process.
Shows signs of using letter-sound approximation in writing, attempting to spell words by principles as well as from memory.
Comments:

(Student self-evaluation form)

Am I developing as an Independent Reader?

Name:_____

Year Level:_____

Year: 19_____

- **Choosing My Books**

  - Do I choose at the right level?

  - Do I choose varied materials?

  - Do I listen to the suggestions of others?

  - Do I use all sources available to me?

- **Reading Independently**

  - Do I enjoy reading quietly?

  - Do I enjoy the daily reading time?

  - Do I choose to read at other times?

  - Do I read different books for different purposes?

  - Do I know what to do when I don't understand something?

  - Do I know what to do when I don't know a word?

Taking Part in Conferences

  - Do I prepare myself for the conference?

  - Do I speak freely about my reading?

  - Can I talk about what the author means?

  - Do I listen to what others say?

- **Activities**

  - Do I complete a variety of activities?

  - Do I work well with others?

  - Are the activities I choose appropriate to what I have read?

- **Share Time**

  - Do I prepare for share time?

  - Has my confidence improved?

  - Do I consider the audience?

  - Am I willing to share with others?

  - Do I help others find out about books?

- **Reading in Social Studies & Science**

  - Do I use non-fiction books when necessary?

  - Do I understand how to read graphs, charts, maps, etc.?

  - Do I know how to use

    a dictionary?

    a thesaurus?

    a set of encyclopedia?

    an atlas?

  - Do I have ways of presenting the information I have read about?

APPENDIX 2

Chart of Comprehension Skills Analysis for the study of Literature based on *The Barrett Taxonomy of the Cognitive and Affective Dimensions of Reading Comprehension* by Thomas C. Barrett
Prepared by Ronald E. Thomas
Teacher Librarian Adviser Camberwell Inspectorate

Literal Comprehension

1   Explicit recognition and recall from memory

	Activities/Questions
1.1 Recognition of detail	• list main characters. • list places in which action takes place.
1.2 Recognition of main idea	• from a selection (chapter or smaller segment). • what did we find out in this chapter?
1.3 Recognition of a sequence	• re-tell incidents in order for a chapter or larger segment. • make a dice game which follows development of plot or sequences or incidents.
1.4 Recognition of comparisons	• similarity/differences between characters and places. • classify good/bad characters, etc. important/unimportant. changing/unchanged.
1.5 Recognition of cause and effect	• why did a character act as he/she did? • what happened when . . .? • why did it happen?
1.6 Recognition of character traits	• how did the author describe the characters? • classify descriptive words used in text. • what type of person was he/she?

Reorganization

2 Reorganization of ideas and information using text verbatim, paraphrased, or in own words

Activities/Questions

2.1 Classifying
- characters, events, things, places, into categories:
  good/bad
  human/animal
  safe/unsafe places
- under headings the children list important words
  People   Places   Things

2.2 Outlining
- organize direct statements or paraphrased statements into outline form — for a chapter or whole story
- readers supply statements, teacher writes them onto cards and files them as a sorting game.

2.3 Summarizing
- condense chapters using direct or paraphrased statements.
- prepare a story board of pictures as an alternative to writing.

2.4 Synthesizing
- describe characters using information from several sections as author reveals more of character traits.
- write Cinquain Verse to describe main characters.

Inferential

3 Student using information/ideas explicitly stated, his intuition and previous experiences as a basis for hypothesis

Activities/Questions

3.1 Inferring supporting detail	• did the author tell you enough about a character for you to know a lot about him?
3.2 Inferring main idea	• why did the author write his story? • what do we learn about the author's thinking? • what is he trying to make us think about?
3.3 Inferring sequence	• what might have happened in the time between two recorded actions or incidents? (time lapses used by author.) • what would have happened if the incident had not ended as it did? • discuss alternative ending of sequences of events.
3.4 Inferring comparisons	• how are characters, places, times different/alike? here — there then — now he — she she — she he — he
3.5 Inferring cause and effect relationships. Character traits. Motivation and interaction.	• why did a character act in such a way? • what influenced their action? • why were they the way they were? • how did a character's actions affect outcome of events?
3.6 Predicting outcomes	• what might happen in next chapter/sequence?
3.7 Interpreting figurative language	• discussion will be required as the story progresses to ensure that all students are aware of concepts. • In discussion groups the leader may re-read some examples of the figurative speech and discuss interpretation.

Evaluative

4 Reading and questioning aims to obtain responses of judgement comparing ideas in story with criteria from external sources (teacher, other written sources) and with internal criteria (readers' experience, knowledge and values).

	Activities/Questions
4.1 Judgements of reality and fantasy	• could this story really have happened? • are people really like this? • could there be a place like the setting? • can the reader relate characters and settings to real life situations? • what other books have you read like this one?
4.2 Judgements of fact or opinion	• is the author trying to sway your thinking? • looking for bias • can reader identify the author's purpose for writing?
4.3 Judgement of appropriateness	• what part of the story best describes the main character, setting? • can reader judge relative adequacy of author's writing? • does the author give us enough information?
4.4 Judgement of worth, desirability and acceptablity.	• was the character right or wrong in what he did? • was his behaviour good or bad?

In this level we are looking for judgements based on the reader's moral code and his value system.

Appreciation

5 Involves all the previous levels and asks for emotional responses to the author's style and technique.

	Activities/Questions
5.1 Emotional response to content.	• how did you feel?
5.2 Identification with characters and incidents • Empathy • Sensitivity • Sympathy	• why did you feel that way? • relate to personal experiences
5.3 Reactions to author's use of language • Style • Imagery	• how did the author make you feel the way you did? • what words did he use? • how did these words help you visualize, smell, taste, hear or feel? • what memorable pictures has the author made?

Bibliography

From: 'In To Books', Ron Thomas & Andrew Perry, Library Advisers, Camberwell Inspectorate, 1981.

APPENDIX 3

Literacy Standards in Australia

1 Little, Graham, 'Standards of Literacy in Australia' in Burnes, French & Moore (eds.) *Literacy: Strategies and Perspectives* Australian Reading Association, 1985, pp.205-6.

2 Power, Colin, 'Reactions to a Report on Reading Standards', *Australian Journal of Reading*, 2, 2, June 1979, 92-95.

3 Hay, John, 'Indices of Literacy' *Australian Journal of Reading* 3, 1, March 1980, 9-12, (This journal has 'standards of literacy' as its focus throughout.)

Standards of Literacy in Australia

Grahame Little
Canberra C.A.E.

We often hear that some child can't read or write well, that some academic received a badly written essay or that some candidates for a particular job or degree do not perform as well as past candidates. Upon such 'evidence' rests the Theory of Declining Standards.

The only pertinent evidence is survey evidence sampling the total population, not isolated cases or segments of the population subject to market fluctuations.

The accompanying table sums up the available survey data on defined standards of literacy over time. It is quite contrary to the Decline Theory. For some skills, standards have risen; for others, they have held. The alleged decline has been diligently sought by appropriate methods, and has not been found.

There is, however, one additional study, a vocabulary test given in 1970 and repeated in 1975 as part of the A.S.S.P. study, which showed some decline. It was probably too short (only about 20 words) to be significant, but even if this study is counted, *the evidence is 44:1 against the Decline Theory.*

A number of points need to be made about false interpretations of the data. It is not the case, as has been alleged, that the data covers only basic skills: it also extends from basic to high-level skills (see 3. and 4. on the accompanying table). It is not the case that the improvement in A.S.S.P. scores can be attributed to non-government schools: the improvement is too great to have been contributed by only a quarter of those surveyed.

It is *not* the case that there is evidence of a decline. It is *not* the case that we do not know whether there is a decline or not. It *is* the case that we know there has *not* been a decline, with standards holding in some areas and improving in others.

Closer study of the surveys reveals *that there are still some sections of the population in difficulties over literacy:* the poor, some migrants, aborigines and the variously handicapped; among the older people, especially women; among the younger, males.

These are the real problems obscured by the illusory problems of a general decline. If we are to solve them it will not be by going back to the imaginary Golden Age, but by taking unprecedented steps to try for unprecedented standards.

Data	1 Censuses	2 The Macquarie Survey	3 Verbal IQ	4 37 Attainment Surveys	5 Australian Studies in School Performance
Standards	Basic: "Able to read and write"	Basic: "Functional literacy", 80% correct on a 44-item test of everyday verbal tasks, a standard met by average child of 10 years 2 months.	Full range: Scores on standardized tests dependent on reading for meaning.	Full range: Standardised ACER tests of word knowledge, speed of reading, reading for meaning, spelling.	Basic: Criterion-referenced tests of basic skills
Population	All over 14 years of age, except aborigines.	A.N.O.P. sample of 2,000 Sydney people over 16 years of age.	All government school students in Years 4 and 6.	Series of state samples, primary and secondary.	Large national samples of 10 and 14 year olds.
Period and Results	1851 c. 67% 1901 c. 75%	Native English Speakers: Over 60 88% Under 30 98% Others: No schooling here 40% Some schooling here 97%	1920's to present. Scores have risen at all points of the scale.	1940's to 1970's (period of maximum immigration). No significant changes. Some tendency towards more higher and more lower scores.	1975 and 1980. Also state retests between these dates. Equal to U.K., U.S.A. and N.Z. Improvement between test and retest.
Source	Census data	J. Goyen, NCTE Newsletter Feb. 1976	N.S.W. Education Department	M. Skilbeck, Education News, 16, 1977	A.S.S.P. publications, A.G.P.S.

In considering evidence of standards over time other than the survey data, the following are worth noting:

- Archives such as those of *The Bulletin,* and any other archives we may have such as parents' letters to schools.
- The statistics for book sales and book use (libraries, etc.) over the decades.
- The movement 'up-market' of newspapers and magazines (a response to rising levels of literacy made by the very newspaper chains which give publicity to the Declining Standards theory).
- The rate of awards of degrees, including Firsts, by the very academics who deplore declining standards.

There is probably a need to gather such evidence systematically, for the Decline Theorists are very persistent, and the issues are too important to be resolved by anything but carefully-gathered relevant information.

Reactions to a Report on Reading Standards

Colin Power
Flinders University of South Australia

Throughout the history of education, individuals and pressure groups have mounted attacks on schools on the grounds that standards in the basic subjects are declining. In Australia, as in most other western countries, we have once again witnessed a resurgence of public concern about reading standards. For the most part, the debates have been ideological and political, the convictions and dogmas of the protagonists rarely being based on evidence. When the findings of research are taken up by a pressure group or the media, the results are frequently distorted to serve political or other purposes. The findings of the report on *Literacy and Numeracy in Australian Schools* (Bourke and Keeves 1977) were no exception in this respect.

Evidence on changes in reading standards across time is exceptionally difficult to find. It is for this reason that the summary of the research into reading standards of Queensland Grade Five pupils (Jacobson 1978) is valuable: it provides important evidence to support or refute otherwise uninformed opinion. Periodic surveys of student achievement in the basic subjects have been undertaken by the Queensland Department of Education in cooperation with the Australian Council for Educational Research since 1933.

The Jacobson paper summarises the results of eight surveys undertaken in Queensland since 1933 (see references), three by ACER and five by the Department of Education. In 1946, 1955, 1960, 1965, 1971, 1976 and 1977, the reading achievements of Grade Five students were surveyed. In the period 1946-1971, students completed Form C of the ACER Reading Test which measures Speed of Reading and Reading for Meaning. In the period of 1971 to 1977, students were given another test, Reading Test QR5 which measures speed, meaning and vocabulary utilising items derived from the New South Wales Basic Skills Battery. In order to make comparisons between performances in the period 1946 to 1965 with 1976 and 1977, scores on the ACER Test Form C were estimated using the correlation between QR5 and Form C.

The results are as follows:

Test	1946	1955	1960	1965	1971	1976	1977
Form C							
Speed	14.0	**	11.9	12.0	11.9	11.3*	11.5*
Meaning	23.0	25.0	22.8	23.3	27.1	26.1*	26.5*
QR5							
Speed					44.1	41.5	42.3
Meaning					26.3	25.2	25.6
Vocabulary					17.9	16.3	16.6
Av. age	11.2	11.1	10.6	10.6	10.5	10.5	10.5

* Estimated score   ** Not administered

Jacobson concludes that, on the basis of the tests used, there has been an increase in the standard of reading for meaning for Grade 5 pupils from 1946 to 1971. In 1977 the results obtained were slightly lower than the 1971 results but were still higher than any other from 1946 onwards. Concomitant with this there has been a significant decline in the average age of pupils tested. There is clear evidence that Grade 5 pupils of the 1970's are attaining a *higher standard of reading*, but are doing so at *an earlier age*, than their peers of the 1930's 1940's 1950's and 1960's. Speed of reading results have remained static over the period tested.

On a national basis, in 1946, Queensland reading standards were considered to be inferior to all other States. The results of the ACER study however indicate that 10 year-olds in Queensland in 1975 were performing above the national average in key areas of literacy.

During the period of time in which these standards have been monitored, there have been significant changes in methods, materials and access to education. This broadening of education has not apparently resulted in a decline in reading standards. Rather, the periodic surveys conducted by the Queensland. Department of Education have shown an increase in *reading for meaning* standards within the State.

Interpretation of the trends revealed in the data is made difficult by the changes in the age and the ethnic origins of the population sampled, the tests used, reading and language usage patterns, and societal expectations of schools. Nevertheless, the conclusions reached by Jacobson do seem to be warranted.

It is interesting to compare the trends reported in Queensland with those revealed in the study of reading standards in England (Start and Wells 1972) undertaken by the NFER. In England, there was a significant improvement in the mean reading scores of 11 and 15 year olds in the period 1948 to 1960. The 1970/1971 figures show that the trends for improvement eased. The improvement in reading performance which appears to have taken place in the late 1950's and early 1960's was maintained in the early seventies.

The research evidence does not support claims that overall reading standards have fallen. Indeeed the level of performance of children today is undoubtedly at least as high if not higher than that which is assumed to have existed in some past golden age. We can and should dismiss ill-founded criticisms from those who make a business out of lamentations and denunciation.

That the proportion of children leaving school who have not yet mastered the reading skills needed for everyday life has not dramatically increased, is, however, no grounds for complacency.

References

Jacobson, J. *A Summary of the Research into Reading Standards of Queensland Grade Five Pupils, 1933-1977*. Brisbane: Queensland Institute for Educational Research, 1978.

McIntyre, G. A. and Wood, W. *The Standardization of an Australian Reading Test*. Melbourne: Melbourne University Press, 1933.

Australian Council for Educational Research. *Summary Report to the Directors of Education*. Melbourne, 1950.

Department of Education, Queensland. *Research Findings in Reading*, Research Bulletin No. 10. Brisbane: Research and Guidance Branch, Department of Education, 1956.

Department of Education. *Two Studies in Reading*. Research Bulletin No. 21. Brisbane: Research and Guidance Branch, Department of Education, 1960.

Department of Education, Queensland. *Studies in Primary School Reading*. Research Bulletin No. 28. Brisbane: Research and Curriculum Branch, Department of Education, 1965.

Department of Education, Queensland. *Survey of Standards of Reading Achievement of Queensland Grade 5 Pupils*. Research Bulletin No. 41. Brisbane: Research and Curriculum Branch, Department of Education, 1972.

Bourke, S. F. and Keeves, J. P. *Australian Studies in School Performance: Volume III, The Mastery of Literacy and Numeracy*, Final Report, E.R.D.C., Report 13. Canberra: Australian Government Publishing Service, 1977.

On Further Examination. Report of the Advisory Panel of the Scholastic Aptitude Test Score Decline. New York: College Entrance Examination Board, 1977.

Report on Aspects of Arithmetic and English in Australian Schools. Melbourne: A.C.E.R., 1949.

Start, K. B. and Wells, B. K. *The Trend of Reading Standards*. London: NFER, 1972.

Indices of literacy

John Hay
University of Western Australia

Throughout history, discussions of contemporary standards of literacy have had in common the presumption that standards are declining and that a concern for this decline motivates these discussions. Although the topic for discussion is *What's happening to standards?*, the media has presented it as *Why are standards declining?* But it seems that standards of literacy have always been declining. The familiar figure of the wise old man complaining about feckless, illiterate youth is recognisable in Egyptian papyrii of the period ca. 4,000 B.C. By the time of Aristotle, this complaint against the young had been generalised to include the people of Greece at large. In a sense, we are rehearsing the same commonplaces. So, the complaints are obviously enduring ones. It may even be part of the condition of literate man to complain about illiteracy as a subtle way of insisting upon his superiority to those less literate than he.

As a student of literature, I am interested in the *ways* in which complaints about declining standards of literacy are used. For example, the person making the complaint characteristically puts himself beyond criticism and measures the distance *beneath* his standards to which the less-literate have fallen, or to which they have risen. His discussion is usually a polemical or argumentative one, but it is conducted by assertions rather than evidence or logical proofs. Finally, the very ambiguity inherent in much of what he says leads him to make broadly inclusive generalisations: *Not only are standards of literacy falling, but morals aren't in very good shape either.* If there was not such a wealth of secular and pre-Christian evidence, I would be tempted to see the discussion of the decline in literacy as part of the evidence of the fall of man. The myth or ideal of the prelapsarian, Edenic world is a powerful one. Adam and Eve must have been literate until they bit that apple, or read the wrong book.

All discussions of *standards of literacy* are vitiated by the slipperiness of the term *standards*. Even lexicographers, those compilers of dictionaries whom Dr. Johnson called *harmless drudges*, have trouble with it: the O.E.D. offers thirty-four meanings and even more variations of these meanings, but suggests that 11.9 is crucial:

> The authorized examples of a unit of measure or weight; e.g. a measuring rod of unit length; vessel of unit capacity, a mass of metal of unit weight, preserved in the custody of public office as a permanent evidence of the legally prescribed magnitude of the unit.

That, of course, is an empirical definition of the sort that we are at home with in the physical sciences. But when such empirical definitions are applied to concepts such as literacy, serious problems arise. As definition 11.12, the O.E.D. offers:

> A definite level of excellence, attainment, wealth, or the like, or a definite degree of any quality, viewed as a prescribed object of endeavour or as the measure of what is adequate for some purpose.

Sub-definition b. focuses the issue more precisely:

> In British elementary schools: each of the recognized degrees of proficiency, as tested by examination, according to which school children are classified.

As an examiner of English in Western Australia for more than a decade, such definitions interest me. Is it, for example, a proof of declining standards that I am quite unable to answer one of the questions on the first-ever university examination of English? "Why is D a perfect letter?" Or, is it a proof of rising standards of literacy that a significantly greater proportion of the population is now staying longer at school and studying English syllabuses that make far greater demands upon their time than was the case in 1914, or even in 1948? During that time Leaving English students in Western Australia had to study only *three* books in their final year. But fifteen-year-olds did have to learn by heart 250 lines of such poems as *Horatius* or *How They Brought the Good News [from Ghent to Aix]*. And for the past few decades, no such task has confronted them.

What is certain is that indices of literacy change from age to age, and even within a single age. It is a paradox, that a person who considers himself highly literate because he has read all of Shakespeare and Dickens can be thought illiterate for his ignorance of Jane Austen and Dostoevsky. Perhaps the most serious problem is that those measures of literacy which we have put our trust in, probably *because* they seem quantifiable, are unreli-

able. Spelling, punctuation and, even, grammar are not the sure evidence of literacy people claim them to be. Poor old Shakespeare could not spell his own name, using at least four variants; Swift and Jane Austen left punctuation matters to publishers' clerks while James Joyce convinces us of the inadequacy of many grammatical and syntactical forms.

Let me conclude with two assertions which space only prevents amplification here. Firstly, it is clear from empirical evidence that there is no convincing proof that standards of literacy in Western Australia are worse than they were twenty-five or even sixty-five years ago. Secondly, empirical measures of *standards of literacy* are profoundly unreliable.

APPENDIX 4

United States Sources for Works Cited in Text

Not all the books mentioned in this text are available in the United States. Many are available, however, and we have organized them in three lists—teacher resources, student materials, and reading programs and series. The teacher resources and student materials lists are arranged alphabetically by author; the reading programs and series list is arranged alphabetically by title.

Teacher Resources

Allen, Roach Van. 1976. *Language Experiences in Communication*. Boston: Houghton Mifflin.

Arbuthnot Anthology of Children's Literature. 1977. Glenview, IL: Scott, Foresman.

Bettelheim, Bruno. 1976. *The Uses of Enchantment: the Meaning and Importance of Fairy Tales*. New York: Alfred A. Knopf. (Also available in 1977 ed. published by New York: Random House.)

Bloom, Benjamin. 1977. *Taxonomy of Educational Objectives: Handbook 1—Cognitive Domain*. White Plains, N.Y.: Longman.

Butler, Andrea. 1984. *The Story Box in the Classroom, Stage 1*. San Diego, CA: The Wright Group.

———. 1984. *The Story Box in the Classroom, Stages 2-7*. San Diego, CA: The Wright Group.

Calkins, Lucy. 1983. *Lessons from a Child*. Portsmouth, N.H.: Heinemann.

Carpenter, Humphrey, and Mari Pritchard. 1984. *The Oxford Companion to Children's Literature*. New York: Oxford University Press.

Clay, Marie. 1979. *The Early Detection of Reading Difficulties: A Diagnostic Survey with Recovery Procedures*. Portsmouth, N.H.: Heinemann.

Dalton, Joan. 1985. *Adventures in Thinking*. From Focus on Writing Package. Crystal Lake, IL: Rigby.

Durkin, D. 1974. *Teaching Them to Read*. 2d ed. Newton, MA: Allyn & Bacon.

Fader, D., et al. 1976. *Hooked on Books*. 10th Anniversary Edition. New York: Berkley Medallion Book.

Gilmour, H., and D. Tyrer. *Reading On*. From Focus on Reading Package. Crystal Lake, IL: Rigby.

Goodman, Yetta, and Carolyn Burke. *Reading Miscue Inventory: Alternative Procedures*. New York: Richard C. Owen.

———. 1980. *Reading Strategies: Focus on Comprehension*. New York: Henry Holt.

Graves, Donald H. 1984. *Writing: Teachers and Children at Work*. Portsmouth, N.H.: Heinemann.

Harste, Jerome, Virginia Woodward, and Carolyn Burke. 1984. *Language Stories and Literacy Lessons*. Portsmouth, N.H.: Heinemann.

Hearne, Betsy. 1982. *Choosing Books for Children*. New York: Dell.

Holdaway, Don. 1979. *The Foundations of Literacy*. Portsmouth, N.H.: Heinemann.

———. 1980. *Independence in Reading*. 2d ed. Portsmouth, N.H.: Heinemann.

Huck, Charlotte S. 1979. *Children's Literature in the Elementary School*. 3d ed. updated. New York: Holt, Rinehart & Winston.

Huttleman, D. 1978. *Developmental Reading: A Psycholinguistic Perspective*. Chicago: Rand McNally.

Johnson, D., and P. Pearson. 1978. *Teaching Reading Vocabulary*. New York: Henry Holt.

Johnson, Terry D., and Daphne R. Louis. 1987. *Literacy Through Literature*. Portsmouth, N.H.: Heinemann.

Leibert, R. (ed.) No Date Listed. *Diagnostic Viewpoints in Reading*. Newark, DE: International Reading Association.

MacGinitie, Walter H. (ed.) 1973. *Assessment Problems in Reading*. Newark, DE: International Reading Association.

Martin, Bill jnr. 1970. *Sounds of Language* series. New York: Henry Holt.

Meek, Margaret, et al. 1977. *The Cool Web: The Pattern of Children's Reading*. Topsfield, MA: Salem House Publishers.

———. 1986. *Learning to Read*. Portsmouth, N.H.: Heinemann.

On Further Examination. 1977. Report of the Advisory Panel of the Scholastic Aptitude Text Score Decline. New York: College Entrance Examination Board.

Parry, Jo-Ann, and David Hornsby. 1985. *Write On: A Conference Approach to Writing*. Portsmouth, N.H.: Heinemann.

Pearson, P., and D. Johnson. 1978. *Teaching Reading Comprehension*. New York: Henry Holt.

Polette, Nancy, and Marjorie Hamlin. 1980. *Exploring Books with Gifted Children*. Littleton, CO: Libraries Unlimited.

Sloan, P., and R. Latham. 1981. *Teaching Reading Is. . . .* From Focus On Reading Package. Crystal Lake, IL: Rigby.

Smith, Frank. 1986. *Reading*. 2d ed. New York: Cambridge University Press.

Stauffer, Russell. 1970. *The Language-Experience Approach to the Teaching of Reading*. New York: Harper & Row.

Strang, R. No Date Listed. *Reading Diagnosis and Remediation*. Newark, DE: International Reading Association.

Sutherland, Zena, and M. Arbuthnot. 1977. *Children and Books*. 5th ed. Glenview, IL: Scott, Foresman.

Tough, Joan. 1983. *Listening to Children Talking: A Guide to the Appraisal of Children's Talking*. Portsmouth, N.H.: Heinemann.

———. 1985. *Talking and Learning*. Portsmouth, N.H.: Heinemann.

Turbill, Jan, and Andrea Butler. 1987. *Towards a Reading-Writing Classroom*. Portsmouth, N.H.: Heinemann.

Trelease, Jim. 1985. *The Read-Aloud Handbook*. rev. ed. New York: Penguin.

Student Materials

Aiken, Joan. 1986. *The Kingdom Under the Sea*. Puffin Storybook Series. New York: Penguin.

———. 1987. *The Wolves of Willoughby Chase*. New York: Dell.

Alexander, Sue. 1976. *Witch, Goblin, and Sometimes Ghost: Six Read-Alone Stories*. New York: Pantheon.

Aliki. 1966. *Keep Your Mouth Closed, Dear*. New York: Dial Books for Young Readers.

Allen, Pamela. 1984. *Berti and the Bear*. New York: Putnam.

———. 1983. *Who Sank the Boat?* New York: Putnam. (Also available in 1987 ed. published by Crystal Lake, IL: Rigby.)

Allsburg, Chris Van. 1981. *Jumanji*. Boston: Houghton Mifflin.

———. 1983. *The Wreck of the Zephyr*. Boston: Houghton Mifflin.

Andersen, Hans Christian. 1987. *The Little Match Girl*. New York: Putnam.

Arbuthnot Anthology of Children's Literature. 1977. Glenview, IL: Scott, Foresman.

Armitage, Ronda. 1979. *The Lighthouse Keeper's Lunch*. Bergenfield, N.J.: Andre Deutsch.

Armstrong, William H. 1969. *Sounder*. New York: Harper Junior Books. Reprint of 1969 ed. 1987. New York: ABC-Clio.

Babbitt, Natalie. 1975. *Tuck Everlasting*. New York: Farrar, Straus & Giroux. Reprint of 1975 ed. 1987. New York: ABC-Clio.

Baker, Jeannie. 1984. *Home in the Sky*. New York: Greenwillow.

Barrett, Judith. 1970. *Animals Should Definitely NOT Wear Clothing*. Atheneum Children's Books. New York: Macmillan.

Berenstain, Stanley, and Janice Berenstain. 1971. *Bears in the Night*. Bright & Early Book. New York: Random House.

Blaine, Margo. 1980. *The Terrible Thing that Happened at Our House*. Reprint of 1975 ed. New York: Macmillan.

Blume, Judy. 1985. *Freckle Juice*. Reprint of 1971 ed. New York: Macmillan. (Also available in 1986 ed. published by New York: Dell.)

————. 1980. *Superfudge*. New York: Dutton. (Also available in 1986 edition published by New York: Dell.)

————. 1972. *Tales of a Fourth Grade Nothing*. New York: Dutton. Reprint of 1972 ed. 1987. New York: ABC-Clio. (Also available in 1986 ed. published by New York: Dell.)

Bridwell, Norman. 1985. *Clifford at the Circus*. New York: Scholastic.

————. 1984–1986. *Clifford* Books. New York: Scholastic.

Briggs, Raymond. 1985. *The Tin-Pot Foreign General and the Old Iron Woman*. Boston: Little, Brown.

————. 1982. *When the Wind Blows*. New York: Schocken Books.

Brink, Carol Ryrie. 1973. *Caddie Woodlawn*. New York: Macmillan.

Brown, Jeff. 1964. *Flat Stanley*. New York: Harper Junior Books.

Brown, Ruth. 1981. *A Dark, Dark Tale*. New York: Dial Books for Young Readers.

————. 1983. *If at First You Do Not See*. New York: Holt, Rinehart & Winston.

Byars, Betsy. 1980. *The Eighteenth Emergency*. New York: Avon. (Also available in 1981 ed. published by Puffin Books. New York: Penguin.)

————. 1975. *The Midnight Fox*. New York: Avon. (Also available in 1981 ed. published by Puffin Story Books Series. New York: Penguin.)

Cairns, Scharlaine. 1987. *Oh No!* Crystal Lake, IL: Rigby.

Carle, Eric. 1981. *The Very Hungry Caterpillar*. (Also available in 1986 miniature ed.) New York: Putnam.

Chaucer, Geoffrey. 1982. *Chanticleer and the Fox*. Illustrated by Barbara Cooney. Crowell Junior Books. New York: Harper Junior Books.

Cleary, Beverly. 1957. *Henry and the Paper Route*. New York: William Morrow. (Also available in 1980 ed. published by New York: Dell.)

————. 1984. *Ramona, Forever*. New York: Morrow Junior Books. (Also available in 1985 ed. published by New York: Dell.)

Cole, Babette. 1986. *The Trouble with Mom*. New York: Putnam.

Cooper, Susan. 1973. *The Dark is Rising*. New York: Macmillan.

Cowley, Joy. 1987. *Mrs. Wishy-Washy*. San Diego, CA: The Wright Group.

Crews, Donald. 1982. *Carousel*. New York: Greenwillow.

————. 1978. *Freight Train*. New York: Greenwillow. (Also available in 1985 ed. published by Puffin Books. New York: Penguin.)

————. 1980. *Truck*. New York: Greenwillow. (Also available in 1985 ed. published by Puffin Books. New York: Penguin.)

Dahl, Roald. 1982. *The BFG*. New York: Farrar, Straus & Giroux.

————. 1978. *Fantastic Mr. Fox*. Skylark Books. New York: Bantam. (Also available in 1986 ed. published by New York: Alfred A. Knopf.)

————. 1982. *George's Marvelous Medicine*. New York: Alfred A. Knopf. (Also available in 1987 Skylark Series ed. published by New York: Bantam.)

————. 1961. *James and the Giant Peach*. New York: Alfred A. Knopf. (Also available in 1981 ed. published by New York: Bantam.)

————. 1966. *The Magic Finger*. New York: Harper Junior Books. (Also available in 1983 Trophy Picture Book ed. published by Harper Junior Books.)

Dahl, Roald, and Quentin Blake (illus.). 1978. *The Enormous Crocodile*. New York: Alfred A. Knopf.

Dahl, Roald, and Mary Tannen. 1981. *The Twits*. New York: Alfred A. Knopf.

Davidson, Margaret. 1973. *Helen Keller*. New York: Scholastic.

Degan, Bruce. 1980. *The Little Witch and the Riddle*. I Can Read Book. New York: Harper Junior Books.

Dickinson, Mike. 1983. *My Brother's Silly*. Bergenfield, N.J.: Andre Deutsch.

Edwards, Hazel. 1986. *There's a Hippopotamus on our Roof Eating Cake*. New York: Holiday House.

Fox, Mem. 1987. *Possum Magic*. Nashville, TN: Abingdon.

Fox, Paula. 1973. *The Slave Dancer*. New York: Bradbury Press. (Also available in 1975 ed. published by New York: Dell.)

Freeman, Don. 1979. *Space Witch*. Picture Puffins Series. New York: Penguin.

Gag, Wanda. 1977. *Millions of Cats*. New York: Putnam.

Gantos, Jack. 1976. *Rotten Ralph*. Boston: Houghton Mifflin. Reprint ed. 1980.

————. 1978. *Worse Than Rotten, Ralph*. Boston: Houghton Mifflin.

Ginsburg, Mirra. 1982. *Across the Stream*. New York: Greenwillow. (Also available in 1985 ed. published by Puffin Books. New York: Penguin.)

————. 1980. *Good Morning, Chick*. New York: Greenwillow.

————. 1976. *Two Greedy Bears*. New York: Macmillan.

Godden, Rumer. 1982. *The Mousewife*. New York: Viking.

Hawkins, Colin, and Jacqui Hawkins. 1984. *Snap! Snap!* New York: Putnam.

Heide, Florence P. 1971. *The Shrinking of Treehorn*. New York: Holiday House.

Hewett, Anita. 1970. *Mrs. Mopple's Washing Line*. Picture Puffins Series. New York: Penguin.

Hill, Eric. 1981. *Spot's First Walk*. New York: Putnam.

————. 1980. *Where's Spot?* New York: Putnam.

Hoberman, Mary Ann. 1982. *A House is a House for Me*. Puffin Books. New York: Penguin.

Hughes, Ted. 1988. *The Iron Giant*. Reissue of 1968 ed. New York: Harper & Row.

Hutchins, Pat. 1976. *Don't Forget the Bacon!* New York: Greenwillow.

————. 1972. *Good-Night Owl*. New York: Macmillan.

————. 1975. *The House that Sailed Away*. New York: Greenwillow.

————. 1980. *The Tale of Thomas Mead*. New York: Greenwillow.

————. 1971. *Titch*. New York: Macmillan.

————. 1986. *The Wind Blew*. Picture Puffins Series. New York: Penguin.

Jansson, Tove. 1975. *Finn Family Moomintroll*. Translated by Elizabeth Portch. New York: Avon.

Juster, Norton. 1961. *The Phantom Tollbooth*. New York: Random House.

Keats, Ezra Jack. 1968. *A Letter to Amy*. New York: Harper Junior Books.

————. 1983. *Louie*. New York: Greenwillow.

————. 1987. *Maggie and the Pirate*. Reprint of 1979 ed. New York: Macmillan.

————. 1967. *Peter's Chair*. New York: Harper Junior Books.

————. 1962. *The Snowy Day*. New York: Viking.

————. 1978. *The Trip*. New York: Greenwillow.

————. 1964. *Whistle for Willie*. New York: Viking. (Also available in 1977 ed. published by New York: Penguin.)

Kellog, Steven. 1971. *Can I Keep Him?* New York: Dial Books for Young Readers.

————. 1976. *The Island of the Skog*. New York: Dial Books for Young Readers.

————. 1977. *The Mysterious Tadpole*. New York: Dial Books for Young Readers.

————. 1979. *Pinkerton, Behave!* New York: Dial Books for Young Readers.

Kemp, Gene. 1980. *The Turbulent Term of Tyke Tiler*. Winchester, MA: Faber & Faber.

Klein, Robin. 1987. *Hating Alison Ashley*. Puffin Books. New York: Penguin.

Krasilovsky, Phyllis. 1972. *The Cow Who Fell in the Canal*. New York: Doubleday.

————. 1982. *The Man Who Didn't Wash His Dishes*. New York: Scholastic. (c.o.p.)

LeGuin, Ursula. 1968. *The Wizard of Earthsea*. Boston: Houghton Mifflin. (Also available in 1975 ed. published by New York: Bantam.)

L'Engle, Madeleine. 1962. *A Wrinkle in Time*. New York: Farrar, Straus & Giroux. Reprint of 1962 ed. published 1987 by New York: ABC-Clio. (Also available in 1976 and 1986 eds. published by New York: Dell.)

Lewis, C. S. 1968. *The Lion, the Witch, and the Wardrobe*. New York: Macmillan.

————. 1967. *The Silver Chair*. Collier Books, New York: Macmillan.

Lionni, Leo. 1970. *Fish is Fish*. New York: Pantheon. (Also available in 1987 Children's Paperbacks Series ed. published by New York: Alfred A. Knopf.)

————. 1966. *Frederick*. New York: Pantheon. (Also available in 1987 Children's Paperback Series ed. published by New York: Alfred A. Knopf.)

————. 1979. *Geraldine the Music Mouse*. New York: Pantheon.

————. 1959. *Little Blue and Little Yellow*. New York: Astor-Honor.

————. 1963. *Swimmy*. New York: Pantheon. (Also available in 1987 Children's Paperbacks Series published by New York: Alfred A. Knopf.)

Lopshire, Robert. 1960. *Put Me in the Zoo*. New York: Beginner Books.

McClintock, Mike. 1958. *A Fly Went By*. New York: Beginner Books.

MacDonald, George. 1987. *The Light Princess*. San Diego, CA: Harcourt Brace Jovanovich.

McKee, David. 1985. *The Hill and the Rock*. Boston: Houghton Mifflin. (Also available in 1986 Puffin Books ed. published by New York: Penguin.)

————. 1984. *I Hate My Teddy Bear*. Boston: Houghton Mifflin.

————. 1982. *King Rollo and the New Shoes*. King Rollo Series. Mankato, MN: Creative Educational Books.

————. 1986. *Not Now, Bernard*. Picture Puffins Series. New York: Penguin.

Mahy, Margaret. 1986. *The Great Piratical Rumbustification the Librarian & the Robbers*. Boston: David R. Godine.

Marshall, James Vance. 1980. *Walkabout*. Downsview, Ontario: Monarch.

Miles, Miska. 1971. *Annie and the Old One*. Boston: Little, Brown.

Milne, A. A. 1961. *Now We Are Six*. New York: Dutton. (Also available in 1975 ed. published by New York: Dell.)

Mosel, Arlene. 1968. *Tikki Tikki Tembo*. New York: Henry Holt. (Also available in 1984 ed. published by New York: Scholastic.)

Murphy, Jill. 1980. *The Worst Witch*. New York: Schocken Books. (Also available in 1982 ed. published by New York: Avon.)

Nesbit, Edith. 1986. *The Five Children & It*. New York: Dell.

O'Brien, Robert C. 1971. *Mrs. Frisby and the Rats of Nimh*. Atheneum Children's Books. New York: Macmillan.

O'Neill, Mary. 1960. *Hailstones and Halibut Bones*. New York: Doubleday.

Parish, Peggy. 1983. *Amelia Bedelia*. New York: Harper Junior Books.

Parks, Brenda, and Judith Smith. (Retold by.) 1988. *The Hobyahs*. Crystal Lake, IL: Rigby.

Paterson, Katherine. 1987. *Bridge to Terabithia*. New York: Harper Junior Books. Also available from New York: ABC-Clio.

———. 1979. *The Great Gilly Hopkins*. New York: Avon.

Pienkowski, Jan, and Helen Nicoll. 1976. *Meg and Mog*. New York: Penguin.

———. 1982. *Meg* Books. Puffin Books. New York: Penguin.

Potter, Beatrix. 1984. *Tale of Jemima Puddle-Duck*. New York: Bantam, and Mineola, N.Y.: Dover. (Also available in 1987 ed. published by New York: Simon and Schuster.)

———. 1974. *Tale of Mr. Jeremy Fisher*. Mineola, N.Y.: Dover.

———. 1986. *The Tale of Peter Rabbit*. New York: Scholastic.

Proysen, Alf. 1960. *Little Old Mrs. Pepperpot*. New York: Astor-Honor.

———. 1961. *Mrs. Pepperpot*. New York: Astor-Honor.

Rosen, Michael. 1974. *Mind Your Own Business*. Chatham, N.Y.: S. G. Phillips.

———. 1984. *Quick, Let's Get Out of Here*. Bergenfield, NJ: Andre Deutsch.

Rylant, Cynthia. 1983. *Miss Maggie*. New York: Dutton.

Schick, Elleanor. 1980. *Home Alone*. Easy to Read Book. New York: Dial Books for Young Readers.

Sendak, Maurice. 1963. *Where the Wild Things Are*. New York: Harper Junior Books.

Serrailler, Ian. 1959. *The Silver Sword*. Chatham, N.Y.: S. G. Phillips.

Slobodkina, Esphyr. 1984. *Caps for Sale*. New York: Scholastic.

Smith, Doris B. 1973. *A Taste of Blackberries*. Crowell Junior Books. New York: Harper Junior Books. (Also available in 1976 ed. published by New York: Scholastic.)

Speare, Elizabeth G. 1986. *The Witch of Blackbird Pond*. New York: Dell.

Spier, Peter. 1978. *Bored, Nothing to Do*. New York: Doubleday.

Steiner, Jorg. *Rabbit Island*. Translated by Ann C. Lammers. Borgh Publications.

Stevens, Kathleen. 1985. *The Beast in the Bathtub*. Milwaukee, WI: Gareth Stevens. (Also available in 1987 Trophy Picture Books ed. published by New York: Harper Junior Books.)

Stevenson, James. 1983. *What's Under My Bed?* New York: Greenwillow. (Also available in 1984 ed. published by Puffin Books. New York: Penguin.)

Stevenson, Robert Louis. 1984. *Treasure Island*. New York: Penguin.

Storr, Catherine. 1979. *Clever Polly and the Stupid Wolf*. Winchester, MA: Faber & Faber.

Taylor, Theodore. 1976. *The Cay*. New York: Avon.

Thiele, Colin. 1978. *The Storm Boy*. New York: Harper Junior Books.

Tolkien, J. R. R. 1984. *The Hobbit*. Boston: Houghton Mifflin.

Vigna, Judith. 1975. *The Little Boy Who Loved Dirt and Almost Became a Superslob*. Niles, IL: Albert Whitman.

Viorst, Judith. 1987. *Alexander and the Terrible, Horrible, No Good, Very Bad Day*. New York: Macmillan.

Vipont, Elfrida. 1986. *The Elephant and the Bad Baby*. New York: Putnam.

Wagner, Jenny. 1978. *The Bunyip of Berkeley's Creek*. New York: Bradbury Press.

———. 1980. *John Brown, Rose, and the Midnight Cat*. New York: Penguin.

Ward, Lynd. 1952. *The Biggest Bear*. Boston: Houghton Mifflin. (Also available in 1973 edition.)

White, E. B. 1952. *Charlotte's Web*. New York: Harper Junior Books.

Wilde, Oscar. 1986. *The Selfish Giant*. Englewood Cliffs, NJ: Prentice-Hall.

Wildsmith, Brian. 1984. *Daisy*. New York: Pantheon.

———. 1969. *The Miller, the Boy, and the Donkey*. New York: Oxford University Press.

———. 1980. *Seasons*. New York: Oxford University Press.

Williams, Jay. 1976. *Everyone Knows What a Wagon Looks Like*. New York: Macmillan.

Reading Programs and Series

Animals on the Move Books. Crystal Lake, IL: Rigby.

Archway Novels. New York: Oxford University Press.

Baa Baa Black Sheep. Big Book/Text Card Series. New York: Richard C. Owen.

The Changing Earth Books. San Diego, CA: The Wright Group.

City Kids and Country Kids Packages. Crystal Lake, IL: Rigby.

Eagle Books. New York: Oxford University Press.

Fables from Aesop. Wright Enrichment Series. San Diego, CA: The Wright Group.

Ginn Reading Program. 1984, 1986. New York: Scholastic.

The Hare and the Tortoise. Story Starter Series. San Diego, CA: The Wright Group.

If You Meet a Dragon. Get-Ready Book, Level 1. From Story Box series. San Diego, CA: The Wright Group.

Look At Books. San Diego, CA: The Wright Group.

The New Ready-to-Read Series. New York: Richard C. Owen.

Once Upon a Time Books. San Diego, CA: The Wright Group.

Read Along Rhythms Big Books. San Diego, CA: The Wright Group.

Read-A-Lot Books. New York: Oxford University Press.

Rigby Theme Packs. Crystal Lake, IL: Rigby.

Story Box Materials. San Diego, CA: The Wright Group.

Story Box—Read Togethers. San Diego, CA: The Wright Group.

Story Box—*Sun Smile*. San Diego, CA: The Wright Group.

Story Box—*Tiddalik*. San Diego, CA: The Wright Group.

Tales from Long Ago Books. San Diego, CA: The Wright Group.

Umbrella Books. New York: Oxford University Press.

Wildsmith, Brian. Picture-Story Books. New York: Oxford University Press.

Windmill Books. San Diego, CA: The Wright Group. (Includes Rhyme and Rhythm Books, and Look and Listen, Sets A & B.)